Assessing**EAP**

Theory and practice in Assessment Literacy

Dr Anthony Manning

Garnet
EDUCATION

Published by
Garnet Publishing Ltd.
8 Southern Court
South Street
Reading RG1 4QS, UK

ISBN 978-1-78260-226-2

British Library Cataloguing-in-Publication Data
A catalogue record for this book is available from the
British Library.

Production
Project manager: Kate Kemp
Editorial team: Clare Chandler, Kate Kemp,
                  Karen Kinnair-Pugh
Design & layout: Neil Collier, Madeleine Maddock
Photography: iStockphoto

Printed and bound in Lebanon by International Press:
interpress@int-press.com

Contents

Introduction

Background

EAP has progressed from a marginal position to become a rich source of empirical research in the field of English Language Teaching (ELT), as well as a major factor in international student success in tertiary education (Hyland & Hamp-Lyons, 2002, pp. 2–3). Confirmation of this situation has been recorded over the course of the last five decades through publications such as Cowie and Heaton (1977), Robinson (1980), Widdowson (1983), Swales (1985), Jordan (1997), Flowerdew and Peacock (2001), Hyland (2006) and Guse and Thornbury (2011), which provide an account of the many and varied approaches, research findings, controversies and increasing levels of expertise that now support EAP teaching contexts.

In recent years, the theme of assessment has been growing in importance in all areas of education, not least in language education. The number of students studying in international contexts through a medium other than their native language has increased rapidly. Consequently, assessment of language as a medium for study in the form of EAP has also become increasingly significant (Blue, Milton & Saville, 2000, p. 7). As a result, assessment can now be seen to be a prevalent practice associated with the teaching and learning of EAP.

What is *Assessment Literacy*?

The term *Assessment Literacy* is now commonly used by researchers in language teaching and general education. This has emerged through a consensus in the field of language teaching and general pedagogy that there is a need to describe what language teachers need to know about assessment matters (Inbar-Lourie, 2008; Malone, 2011; Stiggins, 1991; Taylor, 2009), whether they are involved in the process of selecting, administering, interpreting and sharing results of large-scale tests produced by testing or examination boards, or in producing, marking, analyzing and enhancing in-house or classroom-based assessments (Taylor, 2009, p. 24). It is hoped that this book will assist practitioners in developing and maintaining the quality of assessment procedures, so that stakeholders, in particular test-takers themselves, are not disadvantaged.

In this book, the terms 'testing' and 'assessment' will also be used interchangeably as umbrella terms for both formal and informal procedures associated with gathering language data for the purpose of evaluation (Davies, Brown, Elder, Hill, Lumley & McNamara, 1999, p. 11). Whilst assessment is often accepted as broader in nature and is considered to encompass a wider range of evaluative methods, formal and informal, summative and formative; some individuals consider that testing describes a narrower, more summative and evaluative, activity, relating to scheduled, time-limited assessments undertaken under restrictive conditions (Allison, 1999, pp. 5–6). The view will be maintained that, irrespective of which term is used, the act of evaluating and measuring language ability requires the same level of responsibility regarding purpose, methodology and justification (ibid., p. 6).

About the book

Dr Anthony Manning has taught EAP and managed international pathway programme provision in Higher Education for many years. He is currently Dean for Internationalisation at the University of Kent, where he was also formerly Director of the Centre for English and World Languages. Dr Manning's area of academic specialism is in the teaching and assessment of Academic Skills, English for Academic Purposes and Modern Foreign Languages. Through his career, he has worked as an eternal examiner or adviser for more than five universities, both in the UK and overseas. His Doctorate in Education also focuses on the topic of EAP Assessment Literacy.

References

Allison, D. (1999). *Language testing and evaluation: An introductory course.* Singapore; River Edge, N.J.: Singapore University Press; World Scientific.

Blue, G. M., Milton, J., & Saville, J. (2000). *Assessing English for academic purposes.* Oxford; New York: P. Lang.

Cowie, A. P., & Heaton, J. B. (1977). *English for academic purposes: Papers on the language problems of overseas students in higher education in the UK.* Reading: British Association for Applied Linguistics.

Davies, A., Brown A., Elder, C., Hill, K., Lumley, T., & McNamara, T. (1999). *Dictionary of language testing.* Cambridge: Cambridge University Press.

Flowerdew, J., & Peacock, M. (2001). *Research perspectives on English for academic purposes.* Cambridge: Cambridge University Press.

Guse, J., & Thornbury, S. (2011). *Communicative activities for EAP.* Cambridge; New York: Cambridge University Press.

Hyland, K. (2006). *English for academic purposes: An advanced resource book.* Oxford: Routledge.

Hyland, K., & Hamp-Lyons, L. (2002). EAP: Issues and directions. *Journal of English for Academic Purposes, 1*(1), 1–12.

Inbar-Lourie, O. (2008). Constructing a language assessment knowledge base: A focus on language assessment courses. *Language Testing, 25*(3), 385–402.

Jordan, R. R. (1997). *English for academic purposes: A guide and resource book for teachers.* Cambridge: Cambridge University Press.

Malone, M. E. (2011). *Assessment literacy for language educators* (CAL Digest, October 2011). Washington, DC: Center for Applied Linguistics.

Robinson, P. C. (1980). *ESP (English for specific purposes): The present position.* Oxford: Pergamon.

Stiggins, R. J. (1991). Assessment literacy. *The Phi Delta Kappan, 72*(7), 534.

Swales, J. (1985). *Episodes in ESP: A source and reference book on the development of English for science and technology.* Oxford: Pergamon Institute of English.

Taylor, L. (2009). Developing assessment literacy. *Annual Review of Applied Linguistics, 29*, 21–36.

Widdowson, H. G. (1983). *Learning purpose and language use.* Oxford: Oxford University Press.

Chapter 1: EAP assessment purpose and function

This chapter will:
- explain a range of purposes and functions of assessment in EAP.
- highlight the differences between formative and summative assessment in EAP.

You will have the opportunity to:
- develop an understanding of how EAP tests are used in different contexts.
- understand the importance of creating EAP tests which align with the purposes for which they are intended.

Understanding the assessment objectives

Developing skills in EAP assessment involves knowledge about the purpose and function of testing and assessment. In other words, in order for EAP assessment to be appropriate, suitable assessment tools need to be selected in line with the particular assessment objectives. If this is not the case, then the results of an EAP test may be rendered meaningless.

People's lives can also be adversely affected if the results of EAP tests are inappropriately applied. This is particularly significant in EAP assessment, where test attainment can either grant or block access to study and future career options.

Task 1

- To what extent do you agree that understanding test purpose is important in EAP?
- Think of a situation you are familiar with – related to EAP – where test purpose has not been satisfactorily considered. What were the possible outcomes and how could the situation have been avoided?

Summative and formative assessment

As clarified by Berry (2008, p. 13), assessment is used for a range of different reasons, which can be categorized in a series of differing ways. As in other contexts, in EAP, these can be broadly divided into two areas: namely for drawing inferences related to the performance of individuals or the effectiveness of the education system.

The first area is commonly referred to as *summative assessment*, which returns a mark or grade. The second area focuses on the improvement of learning and the provision of actionable feedback. This is often described as *formative assessment* (Biggs & Tang, 2011, p. 141).

Task 2

- Describe in your own words the distinction between formative and summative EAP assessment.
- In your own EAP assessment, what is the balance in terms of formative or summative approaches?
- Do you think that any one EAP test can be both formative and summative?

Additional purposes of EAP tests

Table 1 extends the basic functions of assessment, as described above, by outlining a series of additional purposes. A model, inspired by Berry (2008), has been adapted to allow for a more specific EAP context.

Table 1: Functions of assessment (adapted from Berry, 2008, p. 13)

Assessment function	Description
Selection, placement and streaming	These EAP tests or examinations are used to determine who will be selected to attend university, or they can also be used to place students in a particular class level. Tests of this nature can also be used to determine whether students require more or less intensive EAP study, or particular EAP modules.
Accountability and achievement	EAP assessments of this nature are used to determine if students have achieved EAP learning outcomes appropriate for particular grades or levels. They could also be used to measure the effectiveness of teachers and institutions in assisting EAP students to achieve intended learning outcomes.

Diagnosis	This type of EAP assessment is used to identify students' particular EAP learning requirements.
Support of learning	This form of EAP assessment is used to monitor the progress of learning; to provide learners with feedback on their learning, to help them improve; to assist teachers in identifying changes to be made in their EAP teaching; to enhance student motivation and confidence by demonstrating progress in EAP skills.

Task 3

- Having consulted Table 1, which of the EAP test functions are you most familiar with in your own working context?
- Are you confident that you are always able to use the most appropriate type of test in the appropriate context?
- Are there any functions listed in Table 1 that you would like to be able to address in your EAP assessment more frequently or by adapting your current EAP assessment tools?

The complexity of identifying EAP test function

Alexander, Argent and Spencer (2008, p. 307) describe the complexities of trying to separate the functions of tests into formative and summative categories. Some summative EAP tests may also have a formative function, whilst a test designed for EAP proficiency measurement may also yield diagnostic information. Crucially, it is important to be clear about test uses so that measures can be taken to ensure that tests are appropriate for the selected purposes. An example is given (ibid.) of the use of a proficiency test for a short intensive pre-sessional EAP course which may not be appropriate if there is not sufficient time for students' overall level of proficiency to improve.

When displayed in this manner, it becomes clear that the task of understanding test purpose is a complex and multi-faceted aspect of developing appropriate EAP assessment tools.

Task 4

- Look at the series of test purpose dilemmas listed in Table 2. What issues in these dilemmas can you identify related to EAP test purpose and function?
- How could the situations in the dilemmas be improved and how could any problematic situations be avoided?

Table 2: EAP test purpose dilemmas

	EAP test purpose dilemmas
1	Senior management has asked your EAP department to use a general pre-sessional EAP achievement test with a group of international nurses who are seeking to find employment at a local hospital.
2	The grades obtained by students on an internationally recognized test of general skills in EAP are used to determine whether students are eligible to join a new Business EAP module.
3	Progress tests, used to help teachers and students monitor EAP skills development during international foundation programmes, are going to be viewed by undergraduate admission tutors to help determine which students should be allowed to join degree programmes.
4	You have been asked by the institution's central admissions team to convert the results of your EAP achievement test into a series of bands which are more commonly used by a well-known and commercially available EAP proficiency test which has quite different marking criteria.

Figure 1 is a revised model developed from Alexander et al. (2008), which summarizes the main purposes of tests, whilst relating them to EAP assessment contexts. The model also highlights typical formative and summative groupings, but acknowledges that some testing circumstances can oscillate between formative and summative purposes.

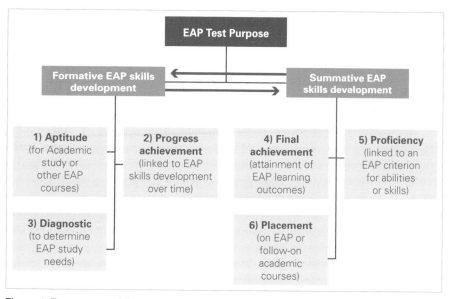

Figure 1: The purpose of EAP assessment (extended and adapted from Alexander et al., 2008, p. 304)

Identifying functions in EAP tests

Task 5

- Read the description of six different forms of EAP test in Table 3 and link them with the six different test purposes in Figure 1.
- In your view, which of the EAP tests have a formative function and which are summative in nature?

Table 3: Descriptions of different EAP tests/assessments

Test example	Test description
Test A	This type of EAP test aims to measure students' levels of ability in EAP. The focus is not on any particular course of study that the student has engaged with. The aim is to determine whether the student's skills in EAP are proficient for a particular purpose. A number of commercially provided EAP tests exist with this purpose in mind.
Test B	Assessments in this category are used to identify areas of strength or development requirements in EAP. In general, this sort of test is used to determine what EAP students' learning requirements are before embarking on a course or programme of study. The results can help the teacher to tailor tuition according to individual students' needs.
Test C	If your institution is able to stream EAP teaching according to differing levels of ability, this type of EAP assessment can assist by identifying which students should be allocated to which particular level of EAP class.
Test D	This kind of EAP assessment or test is more closely related to measuring the impact of a particular course in EAP. Usually the study will have already finished. The objective is to determine the extent to which certain intended learning outcomes have been achieved during the course.
Test E	This kind of EAP test is less common, but could be created to measure students' potential ability in EAP in order to indicate possible achievement in the future on an EAP course or in other programmes in academic study. Such a test could be used to determine whether a student or a group of students have an innate talent or ability in academic writing or other language skills. This information could then be used as part of the process of exploring options for employability or higher education.

Test F	A test of this nature is designed to determine the extent to which a group of EAP students' skills in EAP have developed since the commencement of study on an EAP course or module. Often, this kind of test would be administered during an EAP course. Analysis of the results would also require the teacher to ascertain individual students' learning needs in order to meet the designated learning outcomes.

The EAP test purposes listed in Figure 1 are expanded upon in an alternative taxonomy, provided by Henning (1987, pp. 4–8). Table 4 lists a range of test types as referred to by Henning. These test types have also been extended and applied to an EAP context.

Table 4: EAP test types (adapted from Henning's test types (1987, pp. 4–8))

Objective tests	Subjective tests
This involves comparing EAP test responses with a series of suitable responses, as designated in a key or list of answers.	The awarding of grades or marks for an EAP test through professional judgement.
Direct tests	**Indirect tests**
The testing of EAP skills in an authentic context, such as the assessment of an academic seminar through observing and assessing seminar participation.	Less organic mechanisms for the assessment of EAP skills, such as the use of cloze or multiple-choice questions.
Discrete-point tests	**Integrative tests**
EAP tests which have been created to assess or measure more restricted or isolated EAP skills, such as the use of connective devices or the passive voice.	EAP tests which have been devised in order to assess a series of EAP skills concurrently. This could involve integrated academic reading and writing tests which combine the assessment of research skills and the use of information gleaned from research in academic writing concurrently.

Criterion-referenced tests	Norm-referenced tests
EAP tests which assess EAP students' achievement by comparing learning outcomes achieved with pre-defined assessment criteria. Such criteria are intended to represent the skills required in a general or specific academic domain.	This kind of EAP test is less common, but could be used for the placement or streaming of EAP students into two or more groups. Relative achievement of students through the EAP test could determine which class the student is placed into.
Speed tests	**Power tests**
This type of approach could be utilized with a bank of multiple-choice or 'true or false' questions. Typically, the set of EAP items provided is sufficiently easy so that every student could theoretically answer all items correctly if there were sufficient time available. However, candidates are purposely not given sufficient time and, therefore, students' knowledge and speed of performance are tested.	Sufficient time is given to EAP test takers in order to complete the test. However, the items which are used in the test include a number of complex or difficult EAP challenges and, consequently, not all candidates are likely to be able to respond to each question appropriately or adequately.

Task 6

- With reference to Table 4, which test types do you recognize from your own EAP testing context?
- Which test types would you not usually expect to encounter? Explain why.
- Could you create a useful EAP speaking test by using a set of multiple-choice questions? What are your views?
- Where do you stand on the design and use of integrative tests? Make a list of pros and cons for discrete-point EAP tests and integrative EAP tests.
- What are your views on the use of objective and subjective tests?

Extension activities

The following extension activities can be exploited by colleagues who have additional time to explore and develop the strategies and principles introduced in this chapter.

» With a group of colleagues, undertake an audit of the EAP tests and assessments that you are involved with and check whether you really are using the right kind of EAP test for the purposes that the test is required for. You can start by trying to identify what the true purpose of a particular assessment is and consider whether the type of assessment that you have currently devised really aligns with the purpose or function that the test is set to achieve. You might find that a tool which you are using for EAP diagnostic purposes is actually more suitable for proficiency assessment.

» In order that test takers and other users of your EAP tests are aware of what the test's purposes are – before, during and after taking a test, it is useful to consider any support information that you provide which describes the test – and the functions which it is designed to achieve. In these documents, which can be made available to stakeholders on your website or in hard copy form, you can explain which purposes the assessment is designed for and, importantly, how the test and its results should not be used. This can help stakeholders to understand EAP tests better and, in some cases, avoid misinterpretations of EAP test results.

» It is sometimes the case that when we become familiar with one particular approach to assessment, we may be reluctant to explore other options. Revisit Table 4 and consider whether you could integrate and trial some different approaches in your EAP assessment. For example, you may have always used discrete-point tests to assess academic writing and reading separately. If this is the case, you might like to try the integrated approach to see if this yields different results.

» Try to embed tuition regarding the aims and objectives of your assessments into the curriculum so that EAP students feel confident and aware about why they are being assessed and what that assessment is seeking to measure. Likewise, try to manage the understanding and expectations of other colleagues across your institution or other people who will use your test results. In some cases, you may be able to meet colleagues to explain what your tests seek to achieve and what their limitations are.

Stakeholder support – 'Did you know …?'

Once you have applied the strategies and principles in this chapter to your EAP assessment context, the following information can be photocopied or adapted for use with different stakeholder groups, such as test takers, parents and staff, who are involved in or affected by your EAP testing and assessment. Consider how this passage could be modified or applied in your own working context.

PHOTOCOPIABLE

| Did you know … | that we understand which type of EAP test to use in different situations? |

EAP tests, like other types of assessment, come in a range of different forms (Hughes, 2003). Identifying which type of test to use with a particular EAP student or group of students is important. In the same way that it is important to select the correct utensil or tool for a particular job or task, so it is essential that the correct type of EAP test is selected for the appropriate circumstances. To use an existing metaphor, if you use a sledge hammer to crack a nut, you cannot expect to reach a very satisfactory outcome.

For admissions purposes, we require students to have already obtained an internationally recognized indication of their EAP proficiency. In general, we use placement EAP tests to organize our students into EAP class groups. We create diagnostic EAP tests to determine students' learning needs during our EAP courses. Finally, we also use EAP achievement tests to measure the extent to which students' EAP skills align with the learning outcomes which our EAP modules are based on.

Our tests are also informed by a number of other different assessment options. Our EAP assessments are criterion referenced, based on criteria which have been developed to reflect the EAP skills which we believe that students need to acquire. We build EAP tests which assess both integrated skills, such as reading into writing, and more discrete points, such as vocabulary usage in particular academic contexts.

Above all, we recognize that if the wrong type of EAP test is used in inappropriate circumstances, the results may lead to invalid interpretations, which are misleading for teachers, students and admissions tutors.

References

Alexander, O., Argent, S., & Spencer, J. (2008). *EAP essentials: A teacher's guide to principles and practice*. Reading: Garnet Publishing Limited.

Berry, R. (2008). *Assessment for learning*. Hong Kong; London: Hong Kong University Press; Eurospan [distributor].

Biggs, J. B., & Tang, C. S. (2011). *Teaching for quality learning at university: What the student does* (4th ed.). Maidenhead: McGraw-Hill/Society for Research into Higher Education/Open University Press.

Henning, G. (1987). *A guide to language testing: Development, evaluation, research*. Boston, MA: Addison-Wesley Longman, Limited.

Hughes A. (2003). *Testing for language teachers*. Cambridge: Cambridge University Press.

Chapter 2: Understanding construct validity in EAP assessment

This chapter will:
- introduce you to the concept of construct validity.
- explain how construct validity can assist in improving tests and assessments in EAP.

You will have the opportunity to:
- learn what a construct is in the context of an EAP test or assessment.
- develop strategies for enhancing the construct validity of your own EAP assessments.

The origins of construct validity

More scientific approaches to assessment, including assessment in EAP, can often be linked to the field of psychological testing and the research completed by experts such as Cronbach (1990, p. 192) and Messick (in Linn, 1989, pp. 16–17). These researchers, who have explored the field of measurement in some detail, have had a direct impact on

language assessment, as a result of investigations into reliability and validity. Particularly, familiarity with the concept of construct validity can now be considered as a key skill for EAP practitioners seeking to develop or enhance their own EAP assessments.

The connection between EAP assessment and construct validity is highlighted by Blue, Milton and Saville (2000, pp. 26–27), who share the belief that construct validity is an overarching form of validity, which is crucial to EAP assessment and testing. Construct validity is also described as a key concept or skill for educators involved in assessment (Moss, Girard & Haniford, 2006, p. 116) as an understanding of this area is critical to the building of quality tests and assessments, and the avoidance of the negative influence of poorly operationalized constructs (Fulcher, 1999, p. 226; Messick, 1989, p. 20).

Task 1

- What is a *construct*? Can you think of another word for *construct* which would help in understanding the concept?
- Based on the information provided and your existing knowledge, what do you already understand about construct validity?
- Why do you think construct validity is considered to be so important in test development and what is the relevance for EAP?

Defining construct validity in EAP assessment

Construct validity is a complex concept and it is perhaps unsurprising that some busy EAP teachers may have not had the opportunity to engage with it fully, given time and resource constraints. In the context of EAP, a *construct* could also be described as an area of ability or skill in EAP. Although this definition of the word construct may seem quite simple, often when we come to actually define a particular construct it becomes clear that it is actually quite difficult to achieve. As an example, Figure 1 describes some of the many aspects of the construct of note-taking from academic lectures:

Figure 1: Different aspects of an EAP construct: Note-taking from academic lectures

As can be seen from the aspects of the construct described in Figure 1, the different elements are various in nature and difficult to operationalize in a single test, without leaving out an important element. Indeed, in seeking to define this particular construct, it becomes clear that it includes a number of sub-constructs which are also individually complex to define.

Some other examples of constructs in EAP could include the following:

- The use of noun phrases in academic writing.

- The ability to identify author intent in academic reading texts.

- The capacity to use marketing-related vocabulary in a business-focused presentation.

- The skill of understanding the key stages of a process or method in a scientific demonstration.

Task 2

- Think of a group of students that you teach EAP to and consider one of the key constructs that their assessment focuses on. Try to define this construct and the various aspects which need to be incorporated into the EAP assessment.

Figure 2 shows an example of how one particular construct has been incorporated into an EAP test. In this case, the excerpt is taken from an EAP academic writing paper and the construct which the EAP test writer has tried to operationalize is 'the use of the passive voice in academic writing'.

Question 5

Read the three sentences below and rewrite them using the passive voice, so that they appear more academic in style.

5a)	I undertook this experiment in order that I could determine whether the level of pollution had changed in the stream since I collected my first sample two weeks earlier.	1 mark
5b)	I chose a mixed-methods approach to my research as I felt that I needed to use both quantitative and qualitative data in my investigations.	2 marks
5c)	I interviewed 25 people so that I could obtain a more representative view of professionals in my field.	1 mark

Figure 2: An example of an operationalized construct in an EAP test

---

Task 3

- How well do you think the construct of 'the use of the passive voice in academic writing' has been realized in the set of items in Figure 2?
- What are the possible weaknesses in how this set of items has represented the construct in focus?
- What does it really show if a student gets a high or a low score after completing this set of items?
- How could this set of items be improved?

Evidence to support construct validity

Wigdor and Garner's definition of construct validity (1982) describes construct validity as "... a scientific dialogue about the degree to which an inference that a test measures an underlying trait or hypothesized construct is supported by logical analysis and empirical evidence" (p. 62). This view is supported by recommendations made by Henning (1988), who recommends the empirical validation of EAP tests based on operational test data.

Task 4

- What kind of activities could be involved in the process of validating an EAP test?
- Which questions could be asked in order to deepen the validation process?
- Which pieces of evidence could you collect to support the validity of your EAP testing?
- Have you ever been involved with the process of validating one of your own EAP tests? If so, what did this involve?

Figure 3 provides some examples of evidence which could be used in the process of construct validation for an EAP test item; in this case, the item is an EAP essay.

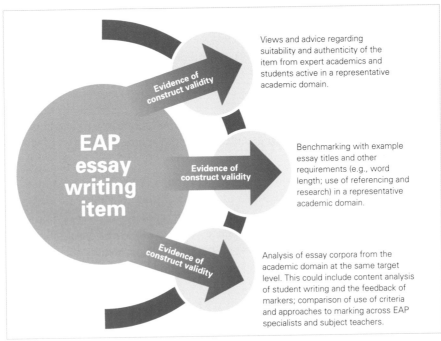

Views and advice regarding suitability and authenticity of the item from expert academics and students active in a representative academic domain.

Benchmarking with example essay titles and other requirements (e.g., word length; use of referencing and research) in a representative academic domain.

Analysis of essay corpora from the academic domain at the same target level. This could include content analysis of student writing and the feedback of markers; comparison of use of criteria and approaches to marking across EAP specialists and subject teachers.

Figure 3: Examples of evidence to support the construct validity of an EAP essay writing item

Task 5

- After looking at Figure 3, can you think of any other types of evidence which could be used in the process of construct validation for this EAP test item?

- Choose another assessment item from your own EAP assessment context and think of examples of evidence that you could find to assist in accurately representing or operationalizing the constructs in your EAP tests.

Construct validity as an overarching concept

In some cases, attempts to explain the concept of validity could be considered overly complex due to descriptions of a range of sub-overlapping forms, such as content validity, criterion validity or face validity, rather than the arguably more unified and overarching description of construct validity, as supported by a number of experts (Henning, 1988; Hughes, 2003; Messick, 1989).

Task 6

- As mentioned, within construct validity, other sub-forms of validity are often discussed, such as criterion validity, content validity or face validity. Before looking at Figure 4, consider what you understand by these terms and how they differ and/or overlap.

Figure 4 highlights some of the complex concepts and considerations involved within validity in the context of EAP. In Stiggins' terms (1995), construct validity can be seen to assist in the process of assessment as it provides a fuller knowledge of what is actually being assessed. With the broader reach of construct validity in mind, McNamara (1996, p. 18) also warns of the dangers associated with restricted views of validity in EAP assessment which do not embrace the fuller breadth of construct validity.

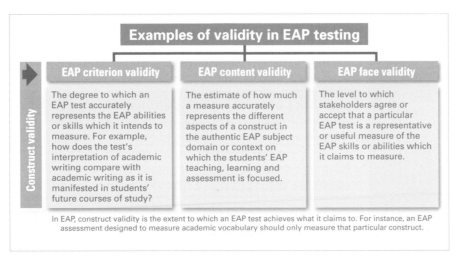

Figure 4: Examples of validity in EAP testing

Task 7

- Consider your own EAP testing context and identify examples of criterion validity, content validity or face validity.
- Do you agree that focus on individual forms of validity could restrict a broader focus on construct validity, which subsumes other forms?

Messick's unitary approach

In terms of a more consolidated view, Messick (1989) is recognized as changing the way in which validity is defined and approached through his particular description of construct validity as a unitary concept with various features. This view prioritizes concern for creating tests which include accurate reflections of relevant constructs, but also draws attention to the appropriate usage of test results, given the consequences for people's lives.

Task 8

- Read the scenarios as described in Table 1 and identify what might challenge the validity of the EAP assessments which have been described.
- How could the assessments or the surrounding situation be improved?
- With a colleague, discuss any similar experiences that you may have encountered in your own work.

Table 1: EAP test validity scenarios

Scenario 1	The syllabus and teaching for Term 2 of Module EAP21 includes a week of tuition, during which, students are taught how to structure and deliver an academic presentation at a British university. At the end of the first term, students also had to complete an assessed presentation which contributes 10% to the same module's overall grade.
Scenario 2	Students in Class A are all taking an International Foundation Programme at your institution. Most students in Class A are getting excellent grades in their three subject modules, including in the lecturers' feedback on their academic writing. However, the grades which the same students are getting in their EAP module are much lower.
Scenario 3	Several students taking Module PM32, part of a pre-master's programme for students working towards postgraduate Management Studies, have complained that their EAP tests are not an accurate reflection of the management skills which they require.
Scenario 4	Science students in your EAP group have complained that your academic writing class is too essay-focused.
Scenario 5	EAP test design and marking at your university is generally given to new members of EAP staff as a training and development opportunity.

A thorough process of validation is likely to be detailed and time-consuming if done properly. However, as a starting point, a series of validity-related probing questions, such as those taken from Messick (1989, p. 16) and adapted for EAP in Table 2, can assist with some initial explorations into the construct validity of an EAP test or assessment.

Table 2: Initial probing questions in the process of EAP construct validation (adapted from Messick (1989, p. 16))

Probing question	EAP example
Does the content of the EAP assessment method adequately match the content and objectives or intended learning outcomes of the EAP programme/ curriculum?	If one of the questions in your EAP test involves testing the use of information taken from lectures, have students been taught how to record and use information collected from lectures? Is the use of information in this way referred to in the learning objectives for this EAP course? In addition, does the assessment question and the test conditions replicate the skill and its reproduction as taught in the classroom?
Are EAP students responding and reacting to the EAP assessment methods and enquiries in expected ways?	As teachers of EAP and other subjects are likely to have experience of students' abilities in use of information drawn from lectures, do the responses provided by students in EAP tests tally with teachers' knowledge of students' abilities as noted in other circumstances?
Does the EAP assessment evidence relate in an expected way to external EAP behaviours in practice?	Are there any benchmarks or examples of EAP in practice which could be gathered to use as a comparator or criterion against which students' EAP test performance – in this case, use of information from lectures – can be measured?
Does the EAP assessment method allow us to investigate EAP student differences due to various educational conventions?	In this case, does the EAP assessment take into account that different subject areas may require information to be collected or applied in different ways?
Is the EAP assessment evidence sensitive to the social consequences regarding its use, such as university entrance or academic progression?	For example, are multiple measures of EAP constructs or skill areas captured to enhance reliability of results? This approach would recognize that basing grades on single samples of performance may be unreliable and, therefore, could lead to poor decisions and possible institutional entrance or rejection.

Task 9

- Select one of your own EAP tests or an example of a commercially provided test that you are familiar with and review it using the questions in Table 2.
- Did you notice anything that could be improved or modified and which might assist in enhancing the validity of the test or items that you reviewed?
- Do you think it is ever possible to say that a test is wholly valid or that a validation process is fully complete?

Extension activities

> The following extension activities can be exploited by colleagues who have additional time to explore and develop the strategies and principles introduced in this chapter.

» Work with a colleague at your own institution or at another institution. Exchange EAP tests or sections of an EAP test and make suggestions on how the construct validity of the assessment could be improved. Use some of the processes noted in this chapter as a starting position.

» Which EAP constructs did you feel could be improved upon in the assessments that you reviewed?

» What did you learn about the construct validity of your own EAP assessment, based on the advice provided by your colleague?

» Based on what you have explored in this chapter, identify which resources you will need to enhance and improve the construct validity of some of your own EAP assessments. You could start by working on one module or one EAP skill area within that module's assessment. Consider what you can achieve over the next term, semester or academic year and make a plan for development and implementation. Remember that, even if you don't have time to develop everything this term or even this academic year, planned and regular improvements can still have an important impact over time.

» In Chapter 3, you will explore the role of test specifications in EAP assessment and consider a framework which you could use yourself for your own EAP tests and assessments. Look at a part of one of your EAP tests and start to define the constructs that you are seeking to assess. Once you have settled on a working definition, keep a record of this information so that you can be sure that when you consult it to develop new test versions, your assessment items achieve your intended objectives.

Stakeholder support – 'Did you know …?'

Once you have applied the strategies and principles in this chapter to your EAP assessment context, the following information can be photocopied or adapted for use with different stakeholder groups, such as test takers, parents and staff, who are involved in or affected by your EAP testing and assessment. Consider how this passage could be modified or applied in your own working context.

PHOTOCOPIABLE

Did you know … **that we aim for a high level of construct validity in our EAP assessments?**

In the process of developing our EAP tests and assessments, we try to make sure that the tests and items which we use are an accurate representation and means of measuring the skills which our students need to demonstrate on their intended future programmes of study.

In order to achieve this aim, we base our assessments on evidence which we have drawn from the contexts in which students will be studying.

This can include investigating the requirements of study programmes across the curriculum, developing assessment tasks which replicate those used in future programmes of study and trialling our prototype assessments with students and staff from representative academic domains.

As academic study is a shifting canvas, our assessments also develop and change along with the different demands placed upon our EAP students and the key skills which university departments require.

Our aim is to teach and assess our students in a manner which allows us to measure and report the skills that they have attained in an efficient, representative and transparent manner.

References

Blue, G. M., Milton, J., & Saville, J. (2000). *Assessing English for academic purposes*. Oxford; New York: P. Lang.

Cronbach, L. J. (1990). *Essentials of psychological testing* (5th ed.). New York; London: Harper & Row.

Fulcher, G. (1999). Assessment in English for academic purposes: Putting content validity in its place. *Applied Linguistics*, 20(2), 221–236.

Henning, G. (1988). The influence of test and sample dimensionality on latent trait person ability and item difficulty calibrations. *Language Testing*, 1(5), 83–88.

Hughes, A. (2003). Testing English for university study. *ELT Documents 127*. Oxford: Modern English Press.

McNamara, T. F. (1996). *Measuring second language performance*. London: Longman.

Messick, S. (1989). Validity. In R. L. Linn (Ed.), *Educational measurement* (3rd ed.). New York: American Council on Education.

Moss, P. A., Girard, B. J., & Haniford, L. C. (2006). Validity in educational assessment. *Review of Research in Education*, 30, 109–162.

Stiggins, R. J. (1995). Assessment literacy for the 21st century. *The Phi Delta Kappan*, 77(3), 238.

Wigdor, A. K., & Garner, W. R. (1982). *Ability testing: Uses, consequences and controversies*. Washington, D.C.: National Academy Press.

Chapter 3: Using test specifications to build EAP tests

This chapter will:
- explain how test specifications can be used in EAP test and assessment design.
- provide you with a framework for the use of test specifications.

You will have the opportunity to:
- apply the theory which supports the use of test specifications to your own EAP assessment context.
- develop a tool which can assist in enhancing the ongoing validity of your EAP assessments.

The purpose of test specifications

In language testing, the term *specification* is used to describe a generative blueprint document through which alternative versions of a particular assessment or assessment task can be created (Davidson & Lynch, 2002, p. 4). As Davidson and Lynch (ibid.) put it, 'a specification is an efficient generative recipe for a test that fosters dialogue and discovery at a higher abstract level than achieved by analysis of a simple item or task' (p. 3).

Ruch (1924) provides an early example of an approach to using test specifications for the purpose of creating more objective assessments or tests. This model allows for flexibility according to the context of particular testing requirements.

Task 1

- Consider how you currently approach the creation of EAP assessments or tests, either from scratch or for the purposes of new versions. What procedures do you follow?
- How do you think using a test specification could contribute to this process? What might be the potential benefits and challenges?

The use of test specifications is also central to some approaches to language test design, such as *The Test Design Framework* (Fulcher, 2010, p. 94). Figure 1 adapts Fulcher's general model for the purposes of EAP. In this model, test specifications are used as a fundamental element of the practice of principled test design. Information which might contribute to an EAP test specification is highlighted.

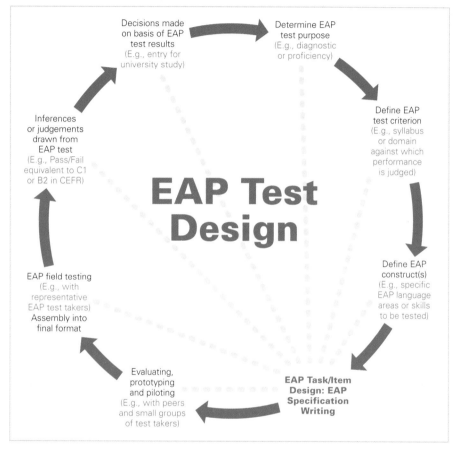

Figure 1: An EAP test design cycle with examples of information contributing to an EAP test specification. Devised and extended with reference to The Test Design Framework (Fulcher, 2010, p. 94).

Task 2

- Do you use/Have you had experience of using test specifications in the process of your own assessment development? If so, how have you done this? If not, why not?

- To what extent does the framework described reflect your own EAP test or assessment design process? What constraints or idiosyncrasies are inherent to your own EAP context?

The importance of test specifications in EAP assessment

Supporting the use of test specifications to facilitate a more scientific and reliable approach to test design is a reoccurring theme in publications relevant to EAP assessment. Such publications include work undertaken by Davidson and Lynch (2002), Fulcher and Davidson (2007) and Fulcher (2006, 2010, 2012a, 2012b). According to Davidson and Lynch (ibid., p. 3) the test specification is the primary tool for language test development. In the view of these researchers, by using a specification, even the lay language assessors can enhance their assessment practice.

Alderson (2000, p. 168) and Alderson, Clapham and Wall (1995) also consider the use of test specifications to be of vital importance to test design, from the perspective of the various stakeholders involved in the process of test design and use. These stakeholders include test writers, test validators, teachers and, certainly, test takers. In addition, research into psychological test construction conducted by Anstey (1966, in Davies, 1990, p. 12) demonstrates that the initial stage of test development requires extensive planning. It is exactly this form of planning which can be recorded in and driven by a test specification. In addition, Davies (1990, p. 12) explains the relevance of psychological testing to the language testing model and supports the use of specifications in the initial planning stage. The need for the use of specifications at the initial stages of language test construction is also advocated by Hughes (2003, p. 26).

Task 3

- What might be the dangers of not using a test specification in developing and using an EAP assessment?
- Who are the stakeholders involved in your context of EAP testing and how might a test specification assist them in teaching EAP, understanding the test and its results?
- How much time is invested in planning and developing your EAP assessments? What hurdles do you encounter and how could they be avoided?

Bachman and Palmer (1996, p. 177) clarify that a test specification can be used for evaluation purposes in order to consider:

- the intentions of the test developer;

- the correspondence between the test and the specification used to develop it;

- the relationship or authenticity of tasks in the test compared to the target language domain.

A prototype test specification was developed by Popham (1978). This has also been adapted by Davidson and Lynch (ibid., p. 14). A further revised model for the purposes of EAP assessment is provided in Table 1.

A model test specification for EAP

Task 4

- Consult Table 1 and note how the framework for producing an EAP test specification is realized in the context of a section of an academic writing assessment.
- Consider a section of one of your own EAP assessments and apply the guidance in the framework from Table 1 to create an initial prototype EAP specification of your own.

Table 1: EAP test specification format (adapted from Popham, 1978 in Davidson & Lynch, 2002, p. 14)

Spec feature	Explanation	Example in an EAP context
Specification number or version code	A number for indexing purposes and version control.	Spec B.1.1
Title of assessment specification	A short label to distinguish between other specs and identify the particular EAP assessment focus.	Academic Connective Devices
Related specifications	List the numbers and or titles of specifications. For example, different items within a reading paper may require individual specifications to allow a description of different skills and constructs in focus.	This specification is linked to other items within Section 1 of EAP Test paper A, which focuses on coherence and cohesion in academic writing. Other items are as follows: • B.1.2: Paragraph structure in academic writing • B.1.3: Introducing and developing an argument in an academic essay Items B2 and B3 are two essay items and Papers A, C and D focus on reading, listening and speaking, respectively.

General Description (GD)	A brief general statement of the behaviour being assessed. This is similar to learning outcomes or objectives.	The aim of this set of items is to assess students' understanding and usage of connective/linking devices which are commonly found and used in academic writing in order to enhance cohesion. Connectives or linking devices can take various forms such as: • simple adverbs (*then, next, yet*) • compound adverbs (*firstly, additionally* or *contrastingly, or moreover, nevertheless* and *furthermore*) • prepositional phrases (*in contrast, on the other hand, in addition*) As a result, EAP items should include a range of different forms of linking devices to ensure that the breadth of the construct is covered.
Prompt Attributes (PA)	Complete a detailed description of what the student will encounter in the test item(s).	In this set of items, students will be given a series of sentences in which connective devices have been replaced with blanks. Students will then have to select an appropriate linking device from a box in order to correctly complete each sentence. In some cases, more than one linking device may be appropriate, but the rubric should indicate that each connective device can only be used once in response to the set of items. One mark will be attributed to each correct answer, with up to ten marks available. No half marks can be awarded.

Response Attributes (RA)	A complete and detailed description of the way in which the student will provide the answer and what will constitute success or failure. There are two types of RA: • Selected response from a series of provided options: Clear details of each available choice. • Constructed response: A clear and detailed response of the type of response students need to provide and which criteria are used to evaluate it.	Selected response: Students should choose an appropriate linking device from the box available, where the devices are randomly arranged. This device should then be written in the gap available in each item.
Sample Item (SI)	An example item or task that reflects the specification.	(1) Microeconomics refers to the study of specific markets, and areas of the economy _____ Macroeconomics focuses on the economy as a whole. **Nevertheless, finally, in contrast, additionally, consequently, However, Furthermore, then, yet, subsequently** Key: The answer to Item 1 could be either 'in contrast' or 'However'. (Note that each linking device can only be used once within the set of ten items.)

| Specification Supplement (SS) | A detailed explanation of any additional required information that is needed in order to create suitable items. This might include academic grammar or vocabulary taught in class or academic sources/texts which should be consulted or avoided. | Please refer to the course materials on page 32 for a list of linking devices which students have been taught. In order to represent the construct of linking devices, the set of items will need to include a rage of different linking devices, such as those listed in GD. |

Developing and applying test specifications

In order for test specifications to be used to their best advantage, an additional recommendation is provided by Fulcher and Davidson (2007), who advise of the importance of allowing specifications to develop through discussion, trialling and piloting in 'a creative, organic, consensus driven, iterative process' (p. 61). This view is reinforced by Jafarpur (2003, p. 72), who recommends the formation of testing-related groups in order that team contributions can be coordinated and recorded so that deviations from test specifications can be avoided. Davidson and Lynch (2002) are also keen supporters of the collaborative and team-based approach to test creation.

With respect to assessment and planning, Bachman (2000, p. 72) recommends 'the development of standards of practice and mechanisms for their implementation and enforcement' (p. 19). However, Jafarpur (ibid., p. 72) warns against the use of specifications in a way which is overly restrictive and risks suppression of writer ingenuity.

Evidently, in reviewing different approaches to the application of specifications, it is widely considered to be the use of a specification per se which is most crucial, rather than the specific manner in which it is employed, as this will vary according to the context and purpose (Davidson & Lynch, 2002, p. 20). This situation may be particularly true of EAP assessments, which may need to assess different skills and language knowledge according to different academic disciplines, task types and assessment objectives.

Task 5

- If you are able to work with a colleague, share your prototype specifications, as developed in Task 4, and attempt to build the EAP question(s) which the spec describe(s). Share your outcomes and critique and revise your respective specifications. This will help you to reach more accurate interpretations of the assessment developer's original expectations. When critiquing your own or others' specifications, consider the following:
  - How easy was the specification to follow and use?
  - To what extent does the item generated from the specification match the original aim and expectations of the test developer?
  - How well do you think the test item and related items represent the construct or language skill area that it has been designed to measure?
  - What could be improved so that others could use your specification to create suitable items?
- How feasible is it for you to work as a team in the process of test development? Make a list of opportunities and challenges. If there are barriers, how might you seek to remove them? If there are key opportunities, what can you do to harness these?
- How could you start to embed the design and use of test specifications in your own working contexts?

Extension activities

The following extension activities can be exploited by colleagues who have additional time to explore and develop the strategies and principles introduced in this chapter.

» With a colleague or a group of colleagues, review a number of past papers or versions of a particular EAP test or assessment that you have used with your students. Using the past papers, try to build a test specification which outlines the intended aims and objectives of the different items in the test. Consider which language skills or 'constructs' the assessment was supposed to measure. Once you have built the test specification, discuss how it could be revised or adjusted in order to measure the key skills in focus more effectively.

» EAP assessments, just like many other activities, can benefit from teamwork and breadth of experience. In order to review one or more of your EAP assessments, try comparing your local approach with that of an EAP team at another institution. You could find a partner EAP department for this activity through an EAP-related professional network or via your external examiner. Exchange one or more assessment tasks with your partner EAP department and try to take into account any constructive criticism that is provided. Challenges which you have found solutions for may be useful benchmarks for another institutions and, similarly, suggestions and advice from a different EAP department could also be beneficial to your working context.

» Work with another institution or EAP department to compare and contrast specifications for particular macro-skill areas, such as reading, writing, listening and speaking. Consider which micro-skills are the target for assessment within the different macro-skill areas which have been identified. What changes do you think could be made and what good practice could you consider transferring to your own test specifications?

» Access and review any available online information relating to a commercially available test in the field of EAP that you are familiar with. Such information can often function in a similar manner to a test specification. Consider how useful you find this information and how it could be improved.

Stakeholder support – 'Did you know …?'

Once you have applied the strategies and principles in this chapter to your EAP assessment context, the following information can be photocopied or adapted for use with different stakeholder groups, such as test takers, parents and staff, who are involved in or affected by your EAP testing and assessment. Consider how this passage could be modified or applied in your own working context.

PHOTOCOPIABLE

Did you know … | **that we use test specifications to guide and support our EAP assessments?**

We believe that it is very important to design and produce EAP assessments in a principled and organized manner. As a result, we practise and advocate the use of test specifications. In many ways, a test specification can be seen to be a blueprint or guidance document for the purpose of ensuring that an EAP assessment measures what is intended or required.

By using test specifications in EAP, the aims and objectives of our assessments can be clearly identified and, where necessary, replicated appropriately when new EAP test versions are being created. As Fulcher (2010) notes:

> When architects begin to design a building, they must have a very clear idea of its purpose. If a client wishes to open a supermarket … I would be rather upset if the architect produced plans for a block of flats. Similarly, the materials needed for the construction of these buildings would be different, and the cost of the buildings would vary accordingly. (p. 95)

As an EAP assessment test-taker or a stakeholder of our EAP assessments, you can learn more about the aims and objectives of our assessments by looking at your course and assessment guides. You can also ask an EAP teacher for further details.

If you would like to find out more about our EAP assessment design process and the specifications which support them, please feel free to get in touch so that we can advise you accordingly.

References

Alderson, J. C. (2000). *Assessing reading*. Cambridge: Cambridge University Press.

Alderson, J. C., Clapham, C., & Wall, D. (1995). *Language test construction and evaluation*. Cambridge: Cambridge University Press.

Anstey. A. (1996) *Psychological tests*. London: Nelson.

Bachman, L. F., & Palmer, A. S. (1996). *Language testing in practice: Designing and developing useful language tests*. Oxford: Oxford University Press.

Bachman, L. F. (2000). Modern language testing at the turn of the century: Assuring that what we count counts. *Language Testing, 17*(1), 1–42.

Davidson, F., & Lynch, B. K. (2002). *Testcraft: A teacher's guide to writing and using language test specifications*. New Haven; London: Yale University Press.

Davies, A. (1990). *Principles of language testing*. Oxford: Basil Blackwell.

Fulcher, G. (2006). Test architecture. *Foreign Language Education Research, 9*, 1–22.

Fulcher, G., & Davidson, F. (2007). *Language testing and assessment: An advanced resource book*. London: Routledge.

Fulcher, G. (2010). *Practical language testing*. London: Hodder Education.

Fulcher, G. (2012a). Assessment literacy for the language classroom. *Language Assessment Quarterly, 9*(2), 113–132.

Fulcher, G. (2012b). *The Routledge handbook of language testing*. Oxford: Routledge.

Hughes, A. (2003). Testing English for university study. *ELT Documents 127*. Oxford: Modern English Press.

Jafarpur, A. (2003). Is the test constructor a facet? *Language Testing, 20*(1), 57–87.

Popham, W. J. (1978). *Criterion-referenced measurement*. Englewood Cliffs, NJ: Prentice Hall.

Ruch, G. M. (1924). *The improvement of the written examination*. Chicago: Scott, Foresman and Company.

Chapter 4: Identifying and sampling the EAP that needs to be assessed

This chapter will:
- introduce you to the challenges involved in sampling academic domains for the purpose of EAP assessment.
- encourage the implementation of certain strategies to assist with the sampling process.

You will have the opportunity to:
- build your skills in sampling, with reference to approaches to needs analysis.
- try out some techniques for sampling the academic domains which relate to your own EAP contexts.

The challenges of domain sampling

Kane (2012, pp. 41–42) explains the challenges presented to educators in domain sampling, or collecting representative examples of target language usage from a real-world context. As Kane (ibid.) explains, identifying the range of performances to include in a target domain, or subject area, and deciding on the emphasis to be given to different kinds of performance tends to be complicated. This is particularly true when the academic domain needs to be used in the development of an EAP assessment.

Task 1

- In your own EAP assessment, how do you normally approach the process of identifying which skills to assess?
- How do you decide on which skill areas within EAP are most important?
- Do you work with academic subject specialists or other EAP teachers with specialisms in particular fields?
- What challenges do you encounter?

In Kane's view, certain key considerations are required when deciding how to approach the sampling process, which is part of the process of identifying what needs to be assessed. These considerations are summarized below.

- When drawing performances from a broadly defined and diverse target domain, the sampling variability is likely to be quite large. This can lead to difficulties when considering the extent to which samples can be used to generalize about wider populations and can also be a source of measurement error.

- When samples are drawn from individuals who are active in the target domain, it needs to be taken into account that performance will be affected by knowledge and skills which are not associated with language. If this is not considered, then it can lead to construct-irrelevant variance (Messick, 1989).

Task 2

- With reference to the summaries above, if you were investigating the EAP skills required for the study of a Business degree, in order to build an EAP test for students seeking to join such degrees in the future, how would you know where to start? How would you identify which aspects of the domain and its constructs should be built into your curriculum and its assessment?

- When you are investigating a subject domain and interacting with subject specialists, how do you distinguish the key EAP skills from other subject-related knowledge or skills?

- How practical or realistic is it for a non-subject specialist to represent the key EAP skills required for study in any given subject domain?

- Where do you stand in terms of focus on teaching and assessing English for Specific Academic Purposes (ESAP) or English for General Academic Purposes (EGAP)?

Stances on specificity and different academic discourses

In relation to EAP, the considerations, as highlighted above, demonstrate that a key aspect of an approach to sampling and consideration of domain relates to the practitioner's stance on the matter of specificity. With this in mind, it is useful to consider debates within EAP which focus on the general or specific purposes dilemma. Robinson (1980, p. 13) and Widdowson (1983, pp. 6–11) did make an effort to describe the great challenge which EAP teachers are confronted with when attempting to successfully and purposefully analyze and describe the spectrum of potential different academic discourses and genres within an EAP classroom. However, notably, little practical solution was proposed.

On the other hand, in the development of ELTS, it can be seen that Carroll (1981) did seek to use an ESP approach to testing (Clapham, 1996) when test versions were developed on the basis of Munby's (1978) Communication Needs Processor model. Furthermore, Swales (1985) offered a number of real-world case studies through his important collection of articles which present a series of different ways in which the various challenges of the science and technology-related EAP/ESP classroom have been met.

Identifying and sampling what needs to be assessed in an EAP assessment

With reference to Table 1, consider the three scenarios related to identifying and sampling what needs to be assessed in certain EAP contexts. How would you advise the EAP professionals mentioned regarding an alternative approach which could yield better results?

Table 1: Scenarios in identifying and sampling what needs to be assessed in EAP

Scenario 1	James has been asked to build an ESAP diagnostic test for students seeking to join a Master's degree in the School of Management. As part of the research, James has interviewed the module convenors of the two core modules from Stage 3 of the school's main Management degree: BM306 Business Law and BM321 Business Strategy. Shortly before the test is administered, James discovers that the Master's degree which the students are hoping to gain admission to is MSc Tourism Management.
Scenario 2	Ella has created an EAP test for a group of actuarial scientists, having interviewed a group of academics from the department and after reviewing a series of reading texts and essay titles which students in the department were provided with. After marking the test and meeting a staff member from the department for a moderation exercise, Ella is surprised to note that the academic doesn't agree with her marking scheme or the judgements regarding the students' level of ability. The academic complains that Ella hasn't approached the marking in the same way that an actuary would and therefore the assessment of the students' language usage isn't very meaningful.
Scenario 3	Simon is teaching a mixed group of EAP students who are working towards study in a wide range of different subject areas. As a result, he has created an EAP achievement test in

which he has tried to embed the core general skills common to a range of subject domains. He has created the test based on what he and his other EAP colleagues deem to be the key general academic skills which students need to apply their use of English to. At the end of the course, Simon sends the results and an overview of the assessment specification to the faculties of Science, Humanities and Social Sciences. Simon is concerned to receive feedback from each faculty claiming that the test's structure isn't representative of the true demands placed upon their students.

Since the 1970s and '80s, controversies have continued to emerge associated with the choices and challenges brought about by choices between EGAP and ESAP (Jordan, 1997; Selinker, Tarone & Hanzeli, 1981; Spack, 1988; Hutchinson & Waters in Swales, 1985; Widdowson, 1983). Jordan (ibid., p. 66) highlights the complex challenges facing EAP course directors, including domain sampling, illustrated in Figure 1 below. This diagram identifies the multi-layered series of considerations which have to be deliberated during the process of creating and delivering EAP programmes. Importantly, these same considerations also have a key impact on the validity and reliability of EAP tests and assessments.

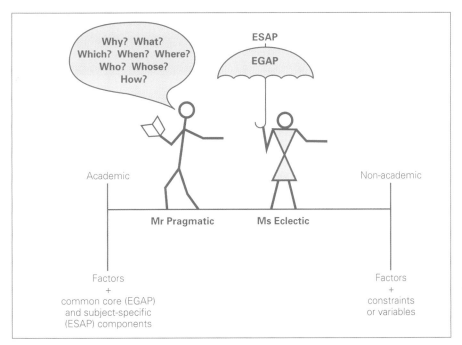

Figure 1: The course design balancing act (Jordan, 1997, p. 66)

From what we have discussed so far, it is clear that choices made by EAP curriculum managers and assessors will have a crucial impact on the sampling process and, ultimately, the EAP test or assessment which is created. However, it should be noted that language testing researchers interested in EAP assessment (Fulcher, 1999; Widdowson, 1983) have criticized the traditional focus and debate in EAP surrounding content and specificity, as they believe it has sometimes caused distraction from what is important in the process of assessment, namely construct validity, as discussed in Chapter 2.

When seeking a framework for identifying assessment requirements in an EAP context, practitioners can make useful reference to research undertaken into learner needs analysis. Although needs analysis was originally conceived in order to service the requirements of English for Occupational Purposes (EOP), this soon moved on to include EAP (West, 1994).

From needs analysis to the sampling process

Table 2, adapted from Jordan (1997), identifies approaches to identifying needs analysis. This has now been supplemented in order to indicate how these needs analysis techniques could be applied to the sampling process for assessment in EAP.

Table 2: Approaches to needs analysis and their application to sampling for EAP assessment

Approach to needs analysis	Description	Application to sampling for EAP assessment
Target Situation Analysis (TSA)	Focus on learners' needs at the end of an EAP course and the benchmark of target-level performance.	Target competencies/ constructs can be used as a criterion for measuring proximity to the EAP domain in focus.
Present-Situation Analysis (PSA)	Focuses on learners' competence regarding skills and language at the beginning of the EAP course.	Understanding of learners' current abilities in EAP can be used to inform a progress test or in the design of syllabus and subsequent achievement testing.
Learning-Centred Approaches (LCA)	A process of comparing target needs with learning needs.	An authentic and representative EAP syllabus and assessment can be devised which provides for the true learning needs of students and devises an appropriate measurement tool.

Strategy Analysis (SA)	This focuses on methods of learning. Learning style refers to the student's preferred way of learning.	To allow for the design of assessments which incorporate assessment types which allow for differing personality types and learning styles.
Deficiency Analysis (DA)	This approach relates existing proficiency to target learner proficiency and identifies weaknesses or deficiencies and determines priorities.	Part of the process of the design of an EAP diagnostic test that can identify skills deficiencies which require prioritization.
Means Analysis (MA)	Investigates the local teaching situation including facilities, teachers and teaching methods to see how the EAP course can be implemented.	Can be applied in the EAP assessment context in order to ensure the best deployment of staff and resources for the purpose of teaching and assessing students with reliability and validity.

Task 3

- With reference to Table 2, which of the analysis approaches best describe the procedures that you have practised in your own working context in order to analyze the academic subject domains which your EAP students are working towards?
- What challenges have you encountered in identifying which EAP skills to teach and to test in your EAP courses and the associated assessment?
- Consider if you could enhance any of your EAP assessments by employing an alternative means of determining the key constructs which need to be assessed and how they are manifested in your EAP assessments.

The approaches to needs analysis which have been listed have relevance to the sampling process, through which key EAP skills for assessment can be identified. In addition to the options provided through these overarching methods, the EAP tutor also has at their disposal various tools to investigate and research the subject domain, which need to inform instruction and the design of assessment. As shown in Figure 4, a number of these mechanisms are also commonly used in the process of needs analysis for syllabus design (West, 1994, pp. 7–8).

- Observation of classes and lectures from the intended academic domain which EAP students are working towards.
- Surveys of students or staff who are currently operating in the target academic field.
- Interviews with academics or representative students from the academic domain.
- Case studies which describe in detail the context and requirements of the target academic domain.
- Review of essays or assignments completed by students in the academic domain.
- Consideration of programme support documentation and any other available documentation which describes the domain, syllabus or curriculum.
- Analysis of learning outcomes and assessment criteria from the intended academic domain.
- Evaluation of feedback provided to students on completion of tests and assessments in the target domain.

Figure 2: Mechanisms for sampling academic domains for EAP syllabuses and assessments

Task 4

- Which of the tools in Figure 2 have you used in the process of researching the academic subjects that your students are working towards?
- How have you used the information that you have gathered to develop your syllabus and EAP assessments?
- Which of the tools listed in Figure 2 would you like to attempt to use? How could this enhance your assessment procedures?
- Are there any obstacles to implementing the mechanisms in Figure 2 for the purposes of researching target EAP domains?
- How straightforward is it for you to gain access to information relating to the subject domains that your students are working towards?
- Are you easily able to collaborate with academic colleagues from the target academic domain?

Weir's research and sampling for EAP assessment

One practical example of EAP sampling in practice, which can act as a useful case study for those working in EAP assessment, relates to the work undertaken by Weir (1983). Weir's research interest aligned with that of Carroll (in Alderson & Hughes, 1981, p. 67), who believed that content validity could be achieved in the testing of EAP through analyzing test takers and their needs, and using this information to determine the content of tests. Central to Weir's research was a behavioural analysis of students' communicative situation in order to determine more accurately what language and communication skills were involved. The main means of establishing content validity was through authentic sampling and representation of the disciplinary domain (Fulcher & Davidson, 2007, p. 6).

Task 5

- Based on what you have learnt from Chapter 2, what is the difference between *content* validity and *construct* validity?

- What concerns might arise if there is too much focus on content validity alone?

After isolating the disciplines and the respective demands of degree programmes most frequently studied by international students at the time, Weir wished to explore the viability of harnessing the results of his study in order to construct a test specification (Waters, 1996, pp. 42–44). Weir aimed to build a test which effectively and more precisely reflected target university communication activities and circumstances under which they were normally performed (Weir, 1988, in Hughes, 1988, p. 46). One major criticism of Weir's focus on the communicative situation is that its preoccupation with content, authenticity and sampling does not address the deeper questions about ability and competence which are now acknowledged as key to construct validity (Fulcher, 1999, p. 223). Furthermore, the difficulty of accurately identifying what constitutes 'authentic situations' was also acknowledged.

Weir's research is relevant to the field of Assessment Literacy as it represents a design for a proficiency test based on sampling conducted through empirical research into student needs. The central view that EAP tests should flow as naturally from needs analysis as the EAP course itself is, however, challenged by Fulcher (ibid., p. 221), who argues that concerns for authentic content should not obscure preoccupation with the main question of how valid inferences are drawn from test scores. Again, this returns the focus back on to construct validity, as discussed in Chapter 2.

Task 6

- Refer back to Chapter 3 on the topic of test specifications. Consider how you would research and design a number of versions of an assessment item for an academic writing task which takes into account the needs of students working towards two or three different subject domains. How might such a test item need to be adapted to take into account how students of different subject domains are required to complete different types of writing task?

- Once EAP study targets have been determined through investigating the academic subject domain and how students are required to use EAP, how can this information be used to help set a benchmark for the learning which has been achieved?

The outcomes-based approach

Research associated with the outcomes-based approach to education and assessment can also offer an important resource to those seeking to identify the key EAP skills or constructs which need to be assessed. In the view supported by Driscoll and Wood (2007, p. 5), by identifying learning outcomes, or stated expectations of what someone will have learnt and how they will be assessed, student-centred learning can be promoted, along with the improvement of curriculum and pedagogy which is benchmarked according to a set of representative criteria. Good practice of this type forms a key feature of many present-day EAP courses which commonly specify intended learning outcomes in order to provide transparent assessment goals (Alexander, Argent & Spencer, 2008, p. 309). Some of the promising practices of good assessment which exemplify the outcomes-based approach are also cited by Driscoll and Wood (ibid., p. 4):

- Assessment information should be provided to students in advance of instruction.

- Students should be able to direct their learning efforts to clear expectations.

- Student progress and completion of learning outcomes are determined by achievement of learning outcomes.

Task 7

- Consider or review the EAP study context of a group of your EAP students and write down an initial list of what you understand to be the intended learning outcomes of the students' study. This is a useful review exercise, if you already have an operational list of existing learning outcomes. If you don't already have access to a list of learning

outcomes for the students in this learning context, you will have to
research the students' learning context more formally, before you can
corroborate the list that you create in this exercise.

- Based on your understanding of the learning outcomes in your new
  list, how well do you think these objectives are serviced by the EAP
  course which the students in question are studying?
- Which changes or enhancements do you feel could be made or need
  to be researched further?

Learning outcomes and Bloom's Taxonomy

Driscoll and Wood (ibid.) also make the point that learning outcomes need to
play a dynamic role in the structuring and development of curriculum; this
view has also led to the use of learning outcomes in syllabus design and for the
basis of assessment. Since its design more than 50 years ago, Bloom's (original)
Taxonomy (1956) continues to be used widely in the process of determining
and measuring learning outcomes in education, including at tertiary level in
specification documents for modules and specifications (Fry, Ketteridge &
Marshall, 1999, p. 33). The focus of Bloom's particular educational research
was to classify the processes involved in learning (Forehand, 2005). With specific
reference to the EAP context, the importance of the processes as identified in
Bloom's Taxonomy is highlighted by Green (2007, p. 48), who explains that, in
academic writing, the stages of the taxonomy are used to both build and assess
student understanding.

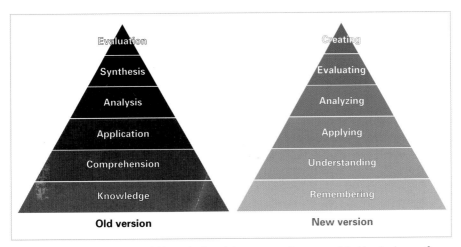

Figure 3: Bloom's Taxonomy (old version) and the new version, as updated by Anderson &
Sosniak (1994, pp. 67–68)

Task 8

- Compare the elements within the versions of Bloom's Taxonomy in Figure 3 and consider how these relate to what needs to be assessed in the context of your own EAP teaching. Which other areas of EAP do you aim to measure in your EAP assessments?
- How do you assess matters such as referencing? How do you manage the balance of assessment of language and skills within your EAP assessments?
- How do you ensure that the way in which you assess language and skills emulates the ways in which students will be assessed in their main courses of study?

With specific reference to the situation facing contemporary students of EAP, Alexander et al. (2008, p. 309) note that the content of university courses has been made more explicit through specifying content in terms of learning outcomes which emphasize what students should be able to do, rather than what is in the syllabus. The impact of the outcomes-based approach on EAP is further highlighted by Sheldon (2004, p. 152), who reiterates that the measurement of EAP skills, in particular academic writing, is best undertaken through an outcomes-based approach, as it prepares students to do and not just to know.

Task 9

- Look at the draft intended learning and assessment outcomes for an EAP module in Figure 4. Suggest how these outcomes, along with the syllabus which they infer, could be improved in order to make them more EAP-focused and comprehensive.

By the end of this Level 3 module in EAP, it is intended that foundation students should:
- be capable of recalling the key function of marketing techniques discussed in the course.
- be able to understand how marketing relates to their degree in Business Administration.
- have acquired academic skills at Level 4 to enable them to use information at degree level.
- be sufficiently proficient in the skills that they have acquired so as to be able to read and write in academic contexts which are relevant to marketing and business.
- be able to interpret and evaluate information which has been drawn from internet sources.

Figure 4: Draft intended learning outcomes for the teaching and assessment of EAP509

Extension activities

The following extension activities can be exploited by colleagues who have additional time to explore and develop the strategies and principles introduced in this chapter.

» Take a section from one of your existing EAP assessments and explore the manner in which you have operationalized the constructs or EAP skills that you are seeking to measure. Ask yourself what evidence you have that these representations of EAP constructs accurately reflect the target domain and, where possible, seek to find evidence from the target domain to support your representation of these EAP constructs. If you can't find this evidence, consider using the information that you have uncovered during this process to rework the constructs within your syllabus and its assessment.

» Work with another colleague from your EAP department and exchange EAP assessments. Review the learning and assessment outcomes which relate to the assessments and consider the extent to which the assessment you are reviewing accurately samples and represents the learning requirements or target EAP usage in the domain which the EAP students are preparing to study.

   » What are the strengths of your current assessment outcomes?

   » Which intended learning or assessment outcomes need to be revised?

   » How could the target domain be sampled more effectively for this purpose?

   » How could other colleagues assist with this process?

» Look back at Figure 2, which provides some of the suggested mechanisms for sampling the academic domains which relate to your own EAP assessment. Identify one of your assessments which you feel could benefit from enhancement and consider how you could deploy three of the techniques in Figure 2 to improve your assessment before its next delivery. Devise a structured action plan so that you have enough time to gather the information that you need and so that this information can be used for the redesign of your assessment.

Stakeholder support – 'Did you know …?'

Once you have applied the strategies and principles in this chapter to your EAP assessment context, the following information can be photocopied or adapted for use with different stakeholder groups, such as test takers, parents and staff, who are involved in or affected by your EAP testing and assessment. Consider how this passage could be modified or applied in your own working context.

PHOTOCOPIABLE

Did you know …

that we pay close attention to academic subjects which our students are intending to study in order to inform the design of our EAP teaching and its assessment?

Our teaching and assessment of EAP aims to develop the skills of our international students so that they are able to communicate and understand the language that is used in the subject that they are currently studying or working towards studying. With this in mind, we believe that it is important for us as teachers and assessors to be aware of the features of the academic subject domains that students are (or will be) studying. By deepening our awareness of the particular ways in which communication skills are used in different areas of the curriculum, we can reflect this in our teaching and assessments.

Whilst some of our EAP teaching is focused on the common core language and skills usage required of university students across a range of subject areas, in other classes or modules, we are able to focus on English for more specific academic purposes. Regardless of the particular approach that we take, we try to learn as much as possible about the study context so that we can create learning and assessment situations which are representative. This way, our teaching and assessment acts as a useful preparation and measure to assist in determining students' needs for future study and, in some cases, students' eligibility for study at higher academic levels.

During the course of the development of our syllabuses and assessments in EAP, we study the exercises, tasks and texts which our students will be exposed to and this helps us to teach and assess their development, which is undertaken through our courses and modules.

References

Alderson, J. C., & Hughes, A. (1981). *Issues in language testing*. London: British Council.

Alexander, O., Argent, S., & Spencer, J. (2008). *EAP essentials: A teacher's guide to principles and practice*. Reading: Garnet Publishing Limited.

Anderson, L. W., & Sosniak, L. A. (1994). *Bloom's taxonomy: A forty-year retrospective*. Chicago: University of Chicago Press.

Bloom, B. S. (1956). *Taxonomy of educational objectives: The classification of educational goals, by a committee of college and university examiners. Handbook 1: Cognitive domain*. New York: Longmans.

Carroll, B. J. (1981). Specifications for an English language testing service. In J. C. Alderson & A. Hughes (Eds.), *Issues in language testing*. London: British Council.

Clapham, C. (1996). *The development of IELTS: A study of the effect of background knowledge on reading comprehension*. Cambridge: Cambridge University Press.

Driscoll, A., & Wood, S. (2007). *Developing outcomes-based assessment for learner-centered education: A faculty introduction*. Sterling, Virginia: Stylus Publishing.

Forehand, M. (2005). *Bloom's taxonomy. Emerging perspectives on learning, teaching, and technology*. Retrieved from http://projects.coe.uga.edu/epltt/index.php?title=Bloom%27s_Taxonomy

Fry, H., Ketteridge, S., & Marshall, S. (1999). *A handbook for teaching and learning in higher education: Enhancing academic practice*. London: Kogan Page.

Fulcher, G. (1999). Assessment in English for academic purposes: putting content validity in its place. *Applied Linguistics, 20*(2), 221–236.

Fulcher, G., & Davidson, F. (2007). *Language testing and assessment: An advanced resource book*. London: Routledge.

Green, A. (2007). *IELTS washback in context: Preparation for academic writing in higher education*. Cambridge: Cambridge University Press.

Hughes, A. (1988). *Testing English for university study*. Oxford: Macmillan.

Hutchinson, T., & Waters, A. (1980). ESP at the crossroads, English for specific purposes, 36. Oregon State University. In J. C. Alderson & A. Hughes (Eds.), *Issues in language testing*. Oxford: Pergamon Press.

Jordan, R. R. (1997). *English for academic purposes: A guide and resource book for teachers*. Cambridge: Cambridge University Press.

Kane, M. (2012). Articulating a validity argument. In F. Davidson & G. Fulcher (Eds.), *The Routledge handbook of language testing* (pp. 34–47). Oxford: Routledge.

Messick, S. (1989). Validity. In R. L. Linn (Ed.), *Educational measurement* (3rd ed.). New York: American Council on Education.

Munby, J. (1978). *Communicative syllabus design: A sociolinguistic model for defining the content of purpose-specific language programmes.* Cambridge: Cambridge University Press.

Robinson, P. C. (1980). *ESP (English for specific purposes): The present position.* Oxford: Pergamon.

Selinker, L., Tarone, E., & Hanzeli, V. E. (1981). *English for academic and technical purposes: Studies in honor of Louis Trimble.* Rowley, Massachusetts: Newbury House.

Sheldon, L. E. (2004). *Directions for the future: Issues in English for academic purposes.* Bern; Oxford: Peter Lang.

Spack, R. (1988). Initiating ESL students into academic discourse community: How far should we go? *TESOL Quarterly, 22*(1), 29–52.

Swales, J. (1985). *Episodes in ESP: A source and reference book on the development of English for science and technology.* Oxford: Pergamon Institute of English.

Waters, A. (1996). *A review of research into needs in English for academic purposes of relevance to the North American higher education context* (TOEFL Monograph Series Report No. 6). Princeton, NJ: Educational Testing Service.

Weir, C. J. (1983). *Identifying the language problems of overseas students in tertiary education in the United Kingdom.* Thesis PhD. London: University of London Institute of Education.

Weir, C. (1988). The specification, realization and validation of an English language proficiency test. In A. Hughes (Ed.), *Testing English for university study. ELT Documents 127.* Oxford: Modern English Press.

West, R. (1994). State of the art article: Needs analysis in language teaching. *Language Teaching, 27*(1), 1–29.

Widdowson, H. G. (1983). *Learning purpose and language use.* Oxford: Oxford University Press.

Chapter 5: Preventing problems in EAP testing before they arise

This chapter will:
- provide a number of mechanisms for enhancing EAP tests before they are operationalized.
- highlight the implications of poor-quality EAP assessment.

You will have the opportunity to:
- explore ethical considerations associated with EAP assessment.
- identify approaches to trialling and piloting EAP tests and assessments prior to their use with students.

The consequences and impact of EAP assessment

Research into the ethics of language testing draws on the methodology of critical social theorists (Bachman, 2000; Lynch, 2001; McNamara, 2001; McNamara & Roever, 2006; Shohamy, 1998, 2001) and builds on Messick's holistic view of validity (Messick, 1989), which includes 'test consequences' and 'social consequences' (p. 20). Messick recognized that the impact of the test on the stakeholders concerned needed to be taken into account when evaluating the validity of inferences drawn from test scores.

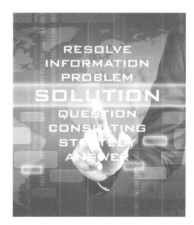

Task 1

- Consider what you think the possible consequences of poorly constructed tests or misinterpreted test results in your own EAP assessment context might be.
- Have you ever experienced a situation related to your own EAP testing where you have been concerned about how the results of your EAP tests have been interpreted or applied?
- Make a list of the possible stakeholders of your EAP tests and how their lives or situations could be affected by poor EAP tests or misconstrued results.

Spolsky (1981) may be considered to be one of the first researchers to refer to the ethicality of test use and to discuss the political purposes for which language testing is sometimes used. In Spolsky's view (ibid., p. 20), language tests should be given a health warning similar to those given to dangerous drugs or chemicals. This is particularly significant in the context of EAP, given the important gate-keeping function which it performs institutionally, nationally and internationally (Flowerdew & Peacock, 2001, p. 192) and the effect that poor assessment or assessment-related decisions can have on people's lives.

Task 2

- Why do you think Spolsky was so concerned about the ethicality of test usage?
- Health warnings are usually confined to poisonous or dangerous substances, such as cigarettes or chemicals. What kind of health warning or usage advice would you attach to an EAP test? Think of some examples and to whom different levels of advice should be addressed.
- The text in this chapter refers to the function of EAP testing which has implications institutionally, nationally and internationally. What are the possible ramifications of EAP testing in these three same spheres?

The stakes are high!

In particular, larger scale standardized tests, which are commercially available, provide a clear example of a high-stakes test with social effects (Spolsky, 2012) given the gate-keeping function which these tests provide in facilitating or withholding access to university study. Indeed, such is the concern regarding test ethicality that some practitioners (Lynch, 1997; Lynch & Shaw, 2005) have designed alternative approaches to language testing in an attempt to avoid some of the practices which they believe to be unethical, and which they perceive to accompany the power imbalance present in some traditional testing systems.

Task 3

- Consider your experience of working with EAP students who have joined your courses, having gained admission through the use of results from a commercially available standardized test. What have you noticed about the results that these students have obtained and how do they affect the decisions that you make on your own courses?
- What are the strengths and weaknesses of the measures of students' skills as provided through the standardized tests?

- How has your understanding of the strengths and weaknesses of these standardized tests influenced your own EAP assessment practices? Which good practices have you sought to adopt, and what have you tried to do differently?

Critical language assessment

Research undertaken by Shohamy (1998, pp. 331–332) shows that there is growing interest in the role played by language testing in society. Consequently, topics such as test ethicality and bias are now being discussed in research, publications and conferences. Shohamy (ibid., p. 332) advocates a critical approach to language testing, which acknowledges that the act of testing is not neutral. Shohamy (2001) probes the socio-political agendas and objectives which language testing practices involve. Similarly, Bachman (1990) supports this view when he refers to the fact that 'tests are not developed and used in a value-free psychometric test-tube; they are virtually always intended to serve the needs of an educational system or of society at large' (p. 279).

As advocated by McNamara & Roever (2006, p. 8), testers need to engage in debate on the consequential application of their tests and need to reflect on test usage after the point of operationalization, in addition to a customary focus on the test development stages. An example relevant to EAP is provided by Shohamy (2001, p. 102), who refers to the impact of an English test in the Middle East used for university entrance and the anxiety which was caused through only minor changes, given the high stakes associated with success.

Task 4

- Think about your own EAP assessment experience. Have you ever felt uncomfortable about how the results of your EAP assessment may have been interpreted or what the results of one of your assessments has indicated? If so, what were the circumstances and how did you seek to avoid the situation in future?
- Typically, how much time do you have to develop EAP assessments and what procedures do you follow to ensure that your assessments have a level of construct validity?
- Read the email in Figure 1 and comment on the ethical implications which it raises and the problems which may emerge for the various stakeholders involved. How could some of these problems have been avoided in advance?

From:	Andrew Mills
To:	Mark Upman
Cc:	Karl Russell

Dear Mark,

I am writing to you regarding a recent decision which has been agreed by the Faculty Board. In addition to the standard assessment which forms part of your existing EAP module, it has been decided that this year's EAP students will also be required to complete a separate EAP test which will need to use the same grading system as one of the commercial tests which the university already accepts. I recall that some of your people are familiar with these external measures, so hopefully you'll be able to rise to the challenge. We haven't referred to the need for this test in students' offer letters for the follow-on courses next year, but the university still feels that it is essential for us to use these new tests from now on. If necessary, we'll write some new offer letters. I realize that the end of year is approaching quickly. The deadline for this new assessment is only two weeks away, but I need you and your team to work with me on this so that the expectations of the Senior Management Team are met.

Although we pushed for you to accept a number of students who didn't technically meet the University's standard requirements at the beginning of the session, we badly need to maintain our international student numbers, so I'm hoping that the results of your new test will not result in a smaller number of students progressing onto their degrees in the next academic year. However, if some students don't get through, who might have been accepted last year, then so be it. We can't afford to have students with poor English at this university.

Thanks in advance for your cooperation.

All the best,

Andy
Faculty Director of Academic Standards

Figure 1: An email from Andrew Mills

Errors associated with the uses to which tests are put can be linked directly with damaging sociological implications and harmful repercussions. The work of Shohamy (1998, 2001) and McNamara & Roever (2006) are particularly relevant in this respect, as they warn of the power of tests and the potential harm which can be incurred. In addition, these risks also resonate with

Foucault's postmodern concerns (Foucault, 1977; Foucault & Gordon, 1980) connected to the interplay between information-seeking and power relations.

With more specific reference to the context of EAP assessment and the need for both EAP practitioners and other stakeholders, including students, to be aware of the societal implications of EAP assessment, Benesch (2001, p. 60) encourages the challenging of conventions associated with EAP through a concern regarding power relations and social justice. Benesch believes that current conditions under which EAP is taught and assessed should be interrogated and probed in the interest of equity and democratic participation, both in and outside of educational institutions. The ultimate aim of Benesch's work is to assist students in performing well in their academic courses (ibid., p. xvi).

Task 5

- Look at the student comments in Figure 2 and consider the problems and ethical situations which they raise.
- Benesch refers to power relations associated with EAP. Are you aware of power relations associated with EAP in your own working context?
- How open are you and your institution to challenges to assessment and grading outcomes lodged by students or other stakeholders?
- Are you confident that the assessment framework that you are required to work within is transparent and robust?

The end of the test for EAP01 last term was not what I had expected at all. The first few questions went well, but then in the second main section, some of us noticed that the questions repeated themselves. I spent ages reading and rereading that section in case I had missed something and, as a result, I wasted a lot of time. In the end, the teacher said that the second main section would be disregarded for everyone, but that didn't help me get back my lost time.

Student 1

In the Reading test, there were some comprehension questions which looked back at the two texts that we had to read. In those questions, we were asked to look back at specific lines in the texts but, when I did that, the content of those lines didn't seem to match the question. That completely threw me and, as a result, I don't think my results were the best that I could have done.

Student 2

> When I got my in-class test back last week, I couldn't quite understand why the answer that I had given for question 14 was given no marks at all. I had a class with another teacher on the same day that I received my feedback and I asked them what they thought and they seemed to agree with me. When I went back to the teacher who had marked my in-class test, he refused to even discuss my results with me and told me that his decision stood.

Student 3

> I've just come out of one of the tests which contributes 20% towards my final grade for my module EAP309. I have really enjoyed this class, but given that the module is supposed to focus on English for Engineering, I don't understand why I had to write an essay which counts for half of the overall marks. In the class, we practised writing reports for several weeks, but we didn't spend very much time on writing essays at all. I thought that this was for a good reason, given that I'm not likely to be writing essays when I go onto my MSc. At the end of the exam, some of us went for coffee and I certainly wasn't the only person to be confused about this situation.

Student 4

> I had my final module exam today for one of the academic English classes which I took and I was really shocked about two things. Firstly, the first half of the test was exactly the same as the practice test that we went over in class last week. Secondly, the multiple-choice questions seemed to be really easy and all the correct answers were either options A or B. I didn't notice the pattern at first, but, after a while, I could see a pattern. I'm sure I'll get a good mark, so I'm not complaining, but it doesn't seem like a very good way to test us.

Student 5

Figure 2: Students' experiences of problems in EAP assessment

Paradigm shifts

Building on the social concerns associated with testing practices, Gipps (1994) recognized the need for a 'paradigm shift' (Kuhn, 1970) in order for stakeholders of examinations to consider assessment in new ways which are suitable for our modern-day purposes and understandings. With this aim in mind, the following measures are suggested:

- moving away from the norm-referenced limiting forces of psychometric models which emphasize ranking;
- producing descriptions of performance which allow for idiosyncratic approaches to learning;

- designing new and richer methods of presenting results using qualitative descriptors, rather than merely figures;
- generating new ways of ensuring reliability and validity due to the changing nature of assessments and their contexts;
- considering ethical issues in the development and use of tests.

Task 6

- Referring back to Gipps' recommendations, what is the difference between norm-referenced tests and criterion-referenced tests? Why might criterion-referenced tests be more appropriate for the EAP context?
- Which of the suggested measures are feasible for you to action or consider in your own EAP assessment context? Which of the suggestions are more difficult for you to implement?

The message needs reinforcing

Despite warnings surrounding the risks related to gaps in practitioner Assessment Literacy and the existence of models of good practice, there still appears to be a sense from critical language testers (McNamara & Roever, 2006; Shohamy, 2001) that an understanding of the power of tests needs to be reawakened amongst language testers. Given that some of the most powerful contemporary tests are frequently used for entry to university and EAP courses, this area of concern should have particular resonance for those involved in EAP assessment.

Task 7

- Reflect on the global nature of contemporary higher education. Given that international students and their parents may seek to invest a great deal of money in education in other countries, what are the risks if measures of EAP proficiency – drawn from standardized tests – are less than trustworthy?
- Given that governmental requirements may require you to use commercially produced standardized tests which have not been designed to fit with your local needs, how can you and your institution seek to understand your students' EAP skills once they have arrived for the start of their degrees or EAP courses?
- Similarly, if in-house EAP assessments delivered by higher education institutions inaccurately block or give access to higher education in the developed world, how might test takers or institutions which receive test takers suffer?

- Consider which outcome is worse: for a student to be accepted for study at a university based on a misjudged assessment of his or her EAP proficiency; or for an institution to reject a student, based on an assessment which has not accurately reflected a student's true level of ability.

The importance of pre-testing

The various stages of piloting and trialling that take place in development, before operational administrations of a test are deemed camera ready, can be described as pre-testing. Skills in this area can be seen to relate directly to the area of Assessment Literacy associated with the avoidance and prevention of test-related problems (Davies et al., 1999, p. 150). As clarified by Bachman and Palmer (1996, p. 234), the amount and kind of pre-testing collection will vary according to the purpose and scope of the test.

Trialling and piloting

Fulcher and Davidson (2007, p. 81) compare the trialling and piloting of language tests to the manufacturing industry and refer to two stages of rapid prototyping, which involves alpha testing and beta testing. Alpha testing refers to the in-house testing of pre-production parts to decide if their design is suitable and to identify and remove any faults through expert judgement. In the context of language testing, this could involve gathering the views of expert colleagues from the field of applied linguistics.

Task 8

- Create a list like the one in Figure 3 of the activities which you practise in your own EAP assessment which could be considered to be alpha testing.
- What other activities could you introduce to test your EAP assessments before you move on to beta testing?

Alpha testing for EAP209 final assessment
- Proofreading and formatting checks undertaken by administrative colleagues.
- Review of test items provided by EAP colleagues in the department. This could also identify matters associated with item discrimination or mark attribution.
- Comments provided by external examiners.
- Consideration of subject specialist comments from colleagues who are active in a representative academic domain.

- Identification of faulty items provided by colleagues or other individuals who have experienced the test under authentic test conditions.

- Judgements relating to the parity between the test specification and the test version.

- Reflection on any previous comments collected from student feedback, based on the evaluation of past versions of the test.

- A comparison, completed by an EAP staff member, of the current EAP test version with previous versions of the EAP test.

Figure 3: Examples of EAP alpha testing

The second stage is beta testing and this involves the external piloting of pre-production items with a representative group of tests takers. Nevertheless, the point is made that, for large-scale tests that will be used to make inferences and decisions about large numbers of individuals, pre-testing is likely to be a more extensive and rigorous process. As many EAP testing contexts fall into the high-stakes category (Alexander, Argent & Spencer, 2008, p. 307), the need for an appropriate amount of pre-testing seems evident in order to avoid any problems which might influence the lives of test takers, should their results on EAP tests not reflect their true abilities.

Task 9

- In a similar manner to the activity in Task 8, look at Figure 4 and list the activities which you practise in your own EAP assessment which could be considered to be beta testing.

Beta testing for EAP209 final assessment

- Analysis of test results using various techniques, depending on the volume of test takers.

- Verbal or written descriptions of test-taker expectations regarding the EAP test, prior to experiencing the test.

- Representative test-taker views on the face-validity of the EAP test on viewing the test paper, but before taking the test.

- Comments provided by test takers based on their actual experiences of taking the test.

- Annotation of the test paper undertaken by representative test takers to note perceptions of difficulty and problematic areas.

Figure 4: Examples of EAP beta testing

Linked to the practices already outlined, Bachman and Palmer (1996, p. 234) suggest three phases of pre-testing, as indicated in Table 1.

Table 1: Steps in pre-testing (Bachman & Palmer, 1996, p. 244)

Step 1	An informal stage where individuals (experts or representative students) and small groups provide qualitative feedback on a test regarding potential problems, specific tasks and instructions.
Step 2	The collection of more quantitative feedback on the test from larger groups of representative students or expert colleagues.
Step 3	A field trial conducted under operational conditions using the same administration procedures as when the test will be given for its intended measurement purposes. This field test stage, however, is only used to assess test usefulness and not to make formal inferences about test takers.

Steps 1 and 2 correlate with alpha and beta testing and Step 3, the field trial, is likely to involve larger-scale piloting of the test with representative test takers and test conditions which mirror as closely as possible those of the true delivery of the test.

Task 10

- Consider to what extent you are able to implement the three stages of trialling and piloting, as described in Table 1.
- If there are certain barriers to one or more of the stages described, consider how these barriers could be obviated.
- One of the most difficult aspects of piloting within the higher education context may be gaining access to representative test takers, given the need for test security and the fact that students may be reluctant to sit additional tests above and beyond their existing requirement. Consider what other mechanisms you may have to access representative test takers or what resources are available to assist you with this.

As explained by Fulcher (2010, p. 159) the process of pre-testing can appear complex. However, in high-stakes situations, it is very important as the process is part of the evidence which can be used to support claims of validity for score meaning. With this in mind, it is clear that understanding the processes involved in pre-testing can be considered an attribute of Assessment Literacy in EAP assessment.

Extension activities

The following extension activities can be exploited by colleagues who have additional time to explore and develop the strategies and principles introduced in this chapter.

» It is often the case that EAP departments are already aware of the flaws or limitations of their own EAP assessment tools. Ask your colleagues to describe the problems that they are aware of in their own EAP assessments and to identify what would be required to improve the situation or to remove the problems completely. With a group of colleagues, try to troubleshoot how you could make some advances with the areas which require most critical address. If additional money or resources are required, consider how you can make a reasoned bid to management for this.

» Based on the dangers of operationalizing tests which have not been trialled or adequately evaluated, try to build a policy for piloting EAP assessments within your department. Create a framework of activity which colleagues can implement.

» With regard to field testing, for security reasons, it is often difficult to identify mechanisms for trialling tests with your own students. Could you trial materials via another university's EAP department or even establish a reciprocal trialling arrangement? You may need to persuade your department to provide funding to encourage student involvement, but the benefits for all stakeholders could be worthwhile.

» With other members of your department, review existing codes of ethics for testing and assessment. Consider how these frameworks can be made central to your team's practice or devise an alternative local good practice guide. Consult the following websites for further details:

http://www.iltaonline.com

http://www.ealta.eu.org

http://www.ukalta.org

Stakeholder support – 'Did you know ...?'

Once you have applied the strategies and principles in this chapter to your EAP assessment context, the following information can be photocopied or adapted for use with different stakeholder groups, such as test takers, parents and staff, who are involved in or affected by your EAP testing and assessment. Consider how this passage could be modified or applied in your own working context.

PHOTOCOPIABLE

Did you know ...

that we make every effort to review and pilot our EAP assessments prior to their usage, so that problems can be identified and test takers are not affected?

EAP assessments are important tools for a wide range of stakeholders, including students, university admissions staff, lecturers and even future employers. Accordingly, we think it is really important to check and review our own EAP assessments as rigorously as possible before we use them for important measurement purposes.

If you were the director of a show or performance, you would likely wish to make sure that the various procedures which contribute towards your production had been checked, risk assessed and appropriately supported before the day of the first live performance. Likewise, you would probably also want to stage a dress rehearsal. If safety measures of this type are not in place, the quality of the performance may suffer and the audience may leave disappointed.

The same logic applies to EAP testing, although, arguably, the stakes are much higher. This is why we try to ensure that activities such as those listed are undertaken, so that the tests which our EAP students sit are able to reveal trustworthy and reliable results.

- We undertake a number of stages of piloting and trialling with smaller groups of expert colleagues and representative students.
- We revise our tests based on stakeholder feedback during the piloting and trialling stages.
- We check the formatting and presentation of our tests for distracting surface errors.
- We field-test our EAP assessments with larger groups of students in order to identify any additional difficulties which can be avoided before operationalizing the test with students who will be formally assessed.

References

Alexander, O., Argent, S., & Spencer, J. (2008). *EAP essentials: A teacher's guide to principles and practice.* Reading: Garnet Publishing Limited.

Bachman, L. F. (1990). *Fundamental considerations in language testing.* Oxford: Oxford University Press.

Bachman, L. F. (2000). Modern language testing at the turn of the century: Assuring that what we count counts. *Language Testing, 17*(1), 1–42.

Bachman, L. F., & Palmer, A. S. (1996). *Language testing in practice: Designing and developing useful language tests.* Oxford: Oxford University Press.

Benesch, S. (2001). *Critical English for academic purposes: Theory, politics, and practice.* Mahwah, N.J.; London: Lawrence Erlbaum Associates.

Davies, A., Brown A., Elder, C., Hill, K., Lumley, T. & McNamara, T. (1999). *Dictionary of language testing.* Cambridge: Cambridge University Press.

Flowerdew, J., & Peacock, M. (2001). *Research perspectives on English for academic purposes.* Cambridge: Cambridge University Press.

Foucault, M. (1977). *Discipline and punish: The birth of the prison.* London: Penguin.

Foucault, M., & Gordon, C. (1980). *Power/knowledge: Selected interviews and other writings, 1972/1977.* Brighton: Harvester Press.

Fulcher, G., & Davidson, F. (2007). *Language testing and assessment: An advanced resource book.* London: Routledge.

Fulcher, G. (2010). *Practical language testing.* London: Hodder Education.

Gipps, C. (1994). *Beyond testing: Towards a theory of educational assessment.* London: Falmer.

ILTA. (2000). *ILTA code of ethics.* Retrieved from http://www.iltaonline.com

Kuhn, T. S. (1970). *The structure of scientific revolutions* (2nd ed.). Chicago, London: University of Chicago Press.

Kunnan, A. J. (2003). *Test fairness.* Paper presented at the European Year of Language Conference, Barcelona.

Lynch, B. K. (1997). In search of the ethical test. *Language Testing, 14*(3), 315–327.

Lynch, B. K. (2001). Rethinking assessment from a critical perspective. *Language Testing, 18*(4), 351–372.

Lynch, B. K., & Shaw, P. (2005). Portfolios, power and ethics. *TESOL Quarterly, 39*(2), 263–297.

McNamara, T. F. (2001). Language assessment as social practice: Challenges for research. *Language Testing, 18*(4), 333–349.

McNamara, T. F., & Roever, C. (2006). *Language testing: The social dimension*. Oxford: Blackwell.

Messick, S. (1989). Validity. In R. L. Linn (Ed.), *Educational measurement* (3rd ed., p. 610). New York: American Council on Education.

Shohamy, E. (1998). Critical language testing and beyond. *Studies in Educational Evaluation, 24*(4), 331–345.

Shohamy, E. (2001). *The power of tests: A critical perspective on the uses of language tests*. Harlow: Longman.

Spolsky, B. (1981). Some ethical questions about language testing. In C. Klein-Braley & D. K. Stevenson (Eds.), *Practice and problems in language testing I* (pp. 5–21). Frankfurt Am Main: Lang.

Spolsky, B. (2012). Language testing and language management. In F. Davidson & G. Fulcher (Eds.), *The Routledge handbook of language Testing* (p. 497). Oxford: Routledge.

Taylor, L. (2009). Developing assessment literacy. *Annual review of Applied Linguistics, 29*, 21–36.

Chapter 6: Encouraging engagement, collaboration and research in EAP assessment

This chapter will:
- clarify the importance of collaboration and research in EAP assessment, as described by experts in the field.
- describe some of the challenges experienced by EAP practitioners in the process of collaborating with colleagues and engaging with research in EAP assessment.

You will have the opportunity to:
- explore opportunities for collaboration with other EAP colleagues and teachers from different subject domains.
- familiarize yourself with a framework for research into EAP assessment.

Barriers and benefits through EAP and subject–teacher interaction

EAP and its teaching and assessment has made a transition from the periphery to become an important aspect of international student success in tertiary education (Hyland & Hamp-Lyons, 2002, pp. 2–3).

Despite the increased prominence of EAP, it should not be overlooked that contemporary opinions continue to differ concerning the role and status of EAP professionals within the university curriculum. Dudley-Evans and St John (1998) believe that working in conjunction with academic schools and departments has the potential to augment the professional status of EAP lecturers. On the other hand, this does not take into account the possible flip-side of such relationships, which risks the classification of EAP professionals as support staff. This situation is described as 'the butler's stance' by Raimes (1991), Bool & Luford (1999, pp. 29–35) and Hyland and Hamp-Lyons (2002, p. 6).

Task 1

- Consider how your own institution or the institutions that you interact with seem to view the status of EAP teachers and assessors in relation to other members of the institution.
- Do you feel that EAP teaching and assessment is a support activity, or an academic activity on a par with the rest of your institution's activity? How does your stance on this matter affect your work?
- Are you able to benefit from access to resources and to engage with research into your practice in a way which can usefully inform your EAP assessment?
- Is there anything you can do to challenge unequal perceptions if they exist?

In a recent research project into EAP Assessment Literacy (Manning, 2013), a large proportion of research respondents recognized the value of interacting with academics in the fields which their EAP students are working towards. This contradicts the concerns described by Raimes (1991). It is also, arguably, in the best interest of students' needs and practitioners' EAP assessment skill development.

Task 2

- Consider the extent to which you personally value and feel comfortable collaborating with other subject teachers for the purpose of designing your EAP syllabus and its assessment.
- How could you extend any collaborative activity which you currently engage in and how could working in new ways with other academics inform your EAP assessment?
- What information would you like to gain access to and how could this improve the construct validity of your assessments?

EAP test development as a 'consensus driven, iterative process'

As discussed in Chapter 5, Fulcher and Davidson (2007) advise of the importance of allowing tests and their specifications to develop through discussion, trialling and piloting in 'a creative, organic, consensus driven, iterative process' (p. 61). This view is reinforced by Jafarpur (2003, p. 72), who recommends the formation of testing-related groups in order that team contributions can be coordinated and recorded. Davidson and Lynch (2002) are also keen supporters of the collaborative and team-based approach to test creation. Whilst Davies (1990) states that 'whether item writing is done by one person or by a working party is incidental' (p. 13), Jafarpur (2003) clearly disagrees and recognizes that, without team contribution, the isolated test or item writer risks adding him or herself as a test facet. Bachman (2000) extends this view and recommends 'the development of standards of practice and mechanisms for their implementation and enforcement' (p. 72).

Task 3

- Based on the recommendations made, to what extent are you able to agree that your own EAP assessment is based on 'a creative, organic, consensus driven, iterative process'? What could you do to change this situation if your current circumstances are less than ideal?
- In relation to Bachman's comments, does your department work according to a set of standards of practice and mechanisms for their implementation?
- If necessary, how could you build a set of standards of practice and what resources could you refer to in order to build these on firm foundations?

Results into EAP assessment practices of staff (Manning, 2013) suggest that interview respondents from the field of EAP, who are engaged in assessment, attach importance to choosing subject matter in tests connected to the academic field of students' study, as well as working in collaboration with academics from the relevant academic fields. Both the theme and magnitude of a series of different item results and data sources have shown that respondents who are active in EAP assessment appreciate the importance of involving academic content tutors in the process of EAP assessment (Davidson & Lynch, 2002; Jafarpur, 2003, p. 72).

Task 4

- Describe some of the positive outcomes which you have reached through collaborating with colleagues from other academic disciplines or indeed other EAP tutors within or beyond your own institution.
- How has your collaborative activity enhanced your assessment practice?
- What implications has this had for test takers or other stakeholders?
- How could you harness this information to make a case for additional collaborative activity in the future?

Working with colleagues from different departments and academic disciplines

Despite the potential benefits of collaborative activity in EAP assessment, one concern which also emerges from the research findings is the reference by a number of interviewees to barriers associated with working with colleagues in other departments across institutions. Nearly 70% of respondents to the research conducted (Manning, 2013) are not able to agree that they frequently work with other academics to help explain EAP. This situation suggests a need to action measures which allow or encourage EAP teachers to play a more active role in liaising with academic colleagues in this manner, so that stakeholders have better understanding of EAP test scores.

Task 5

- Consider possible mechanisms which you and your colleagues could employ in order to work more closely with other academics who are engaged in a range of relevant disciplines.
- What barriers may exist or have previously existed in your own working context? How can these barriers be removed?
- How can improved collaboration be incentivized with the aim of enhancing your EAP assessment practices?
- How could your managers assist in paving the way for this to happen?

Comments drawn from a series of EAP practitioners who are engaged with EAP assessment are listed in Figure 1. These comments highlight some of the varying views which have been expressed.

> It would be good to have a more structured project where it's agreed that because a lot of people are going to work on tests, there needs to be a set procedure. That would help.

> I wonder what pressure it would take for us to actually sit down and work out together what we mean when we talk about assessment … because I think if we seriously did that, I think it would be a tremendously productive process.

> I think I would welcome more people being involved in testing. It all goes back to that community and sort of the collaboration thing.

> The best way is to be able to work with the professionals, although it isn't always the case that lawyers know best about what is the best language to use in their subject.

> I think many universities have EAP and then they have the rest of the university and there has to be a bit more interaction.

> It is important to coordinate things with the department that the students are going on to. Finding what is needed in those departments and feeding that back into both your course design and testing design.

> Ideally, you know, in a perfect world, it would be good to work with the subject teacher.

> There are often difficulties over communication between EAP tutors and departments.

> If you can go up to the department and work something out with them, then that's very helpful for everybody, if they are happy to do that. You know, if you can communicate with that department.

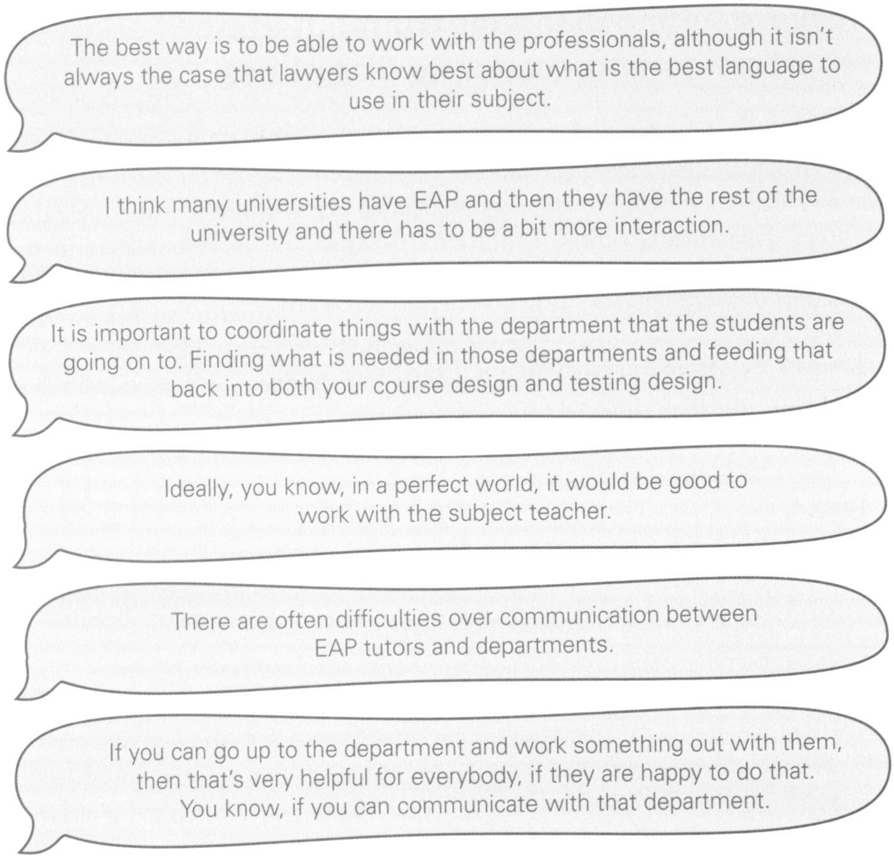

Figure 1: Views expressed by EAP practitioners on the topic of assessment and collaboration

Task 6

- Which of the comments in Figure 1 resonate most with your own experience of collaborating for the purposes of EAP assessment?
- How would you advise the colleagues who have provided the comments in Figure 1 in order to improve the situation they are experiencing or to help remove some of the potential barriers they have experienced?

Engaging in EAP assessment research

In order to consider additional structured and systematic approaches to investigating and enhancing practitioners' EAP assessment, it is useful to refer back to Stiggins (1995) who, in his definition of Assessment Literacy, describes the importance of educators having a fuller knowledge of what is being assessed. Behaviour of this type is also linked to more advanced features of teacher ability, such as those described by Wallace (1991) as the reflective model, combining classroom practice experience with research. In terms of EAP assessment, collaboration with other academic colleagues in different fields can be viewed as part of the process of identifying a clear criterion which can then be harnessed as a means of reference for both test developers and other stakeholders of EAP assessments. This is also part of what Fulcher and Davidson (2007) describe as 'engaging with the disciplines, in order to contextualize instruction and assessment in EAP' (p. 86). Given the important gate-keeping role which assessment within EAP courses undertakes (Flowerdew & Peacock, 2001, p. 192), the author of this resource advocates that research into EAP assessment should be given high priority, despite the fact that it may not always be conducted in a manner which is returnable for institutional research assessment exercises.

Although, in the modern-day university context, research is often associated with large-scale projects, roles with formal research duties embedded within their contracts and institutional ranking procedures, this should not cause EAP practitioners to feel that their own classroom or assessment-focused research is inferior or any less worthwhile. Tests and assessments affect the lives of a wide range of members of an institution and so any well-planned project or investigation which has the potential to inform EAP assessment and its reliability and validity is certainly a meaningful and worthwhile activity.

Task 7

- Consider which particular existing resources you currently use or have used previously to inform your own EAP assessment practice.
- What research projects have you been involved with which might inform your EAP assessment?
- What would you like to know about your own EAP assessment process which you haven't yet been able to explore? How could you make this possible research project happen? How could you gain support from within and beyond your own institution?

A reflective approach to EAP assessment-related research

Building on Wallace's model of the reflective practitioner who combines classroom practice with research, the model in Figure 2 has been devised as an adaptation of Gibbs' (1988) Reflective Cycle to create a framework or guide for EAP, exploring possible EAP assessment research projects.

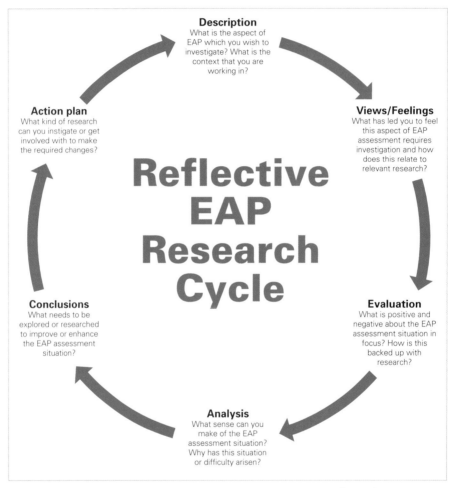

Figure 2: A reflective EAP assessment research model – adapted from Gibb's Cycle

Task 8

- After considering the cycle provided in Figure 2, consider how you could apply this in your own working context.
- Which research project could you instigate or get involved with which could enhance your own EAP assessment practices?

Defining research objectives and research questions

In the process of designing a systematic research project, it is also useful to outline your objectives and to define key research questions. You may also wish to anchor your research by seeking to prove or disprove a hypothesis that you have articulated.

Task 9

- Look at Table 1 and review how the research objectives lead in to research questions and how these fit with the hypothesis which has been provided.
- Consider an area related to assessment in EAP that you would like to investigate and try to build objectives, research questions and hypotheses which could help to anchor and structure your research.

Table 1: Objectives, research questions and hypotheses for EAP assessment research

EAP assessment research topic	Investigating the construct validity of EAP essay questions for students of Art History.
Objectives	To investigate the extent to which essay titles, used in EAP classes for the purposes of developing skills in students of Art History, accurately reflect the constructs referred to in Stage 1 of Art History degrees and are similar to essay titles used for assessment purposes by Stage 1 Art History lecturers.
Research questions	1. How closely do the bank of ten essay titles, used in EAP for Art History EAP603, represent aspects of the syllabus studied by Stage 1 Art History students during the course of their study of the three core modules which contribute to Stage 1 of BA Art History? 2. How similar are the essay titles, in structure and theme, as used in EAP603, compared with the essay titles used by BA Art History core module lecturers?
Hypothesis	The essay titles used in EAP603 do not always accurately reflect the constructs (or aspects of Art History) as introduced in the Art History BA's Stage 1 core modules. The essay titles also do not always compare favourably with the essay titles used in Stage 1 Art History core modules, in terms of both structure and theme.

Null hypothesis (to seek evidence for the rejection of)	The essay titles used in EAP603 accurately reflect the constructs (or aspects of Art History) as introduced in the Art History BA's Stage 1 core modules. The essay titles also compare favourably with the essay titles used in Stage 1 Art History core modules in terms of both structure and theme.

EAP assessment skill development and training

In terms of providing EAP teachers with opportunities for the development of assessment-related skills, Brindley (2001, p. 127) addresses the challenge of assisting language teachers in the development of certain key skills and maintains that there is a lack of prominence attributed to the process of assessment in teacher education courses. In Brindley's view, this, together with the density of language-testing literature, risks alienating the everyday classroom practitioner. Consequently, a situation can arise whereby some teachers engaged in the process of language testing may feel that it is an excessively complex practice which is accessible only to experts (Taylor, 2009, p. 21). Indeed, it may sometimes be the case that assessment-related development opportunities are considered off-putting to some potential users due to a perception that they are likely to be excessively technical (Stiggins, 1991). Popham (2009) also describes how beliefs linking assessment with expertise can be demotivating for some language-teaching professionals. Brown and Bailey's (2008) investigations into the structure of existing training courses for teachers in language testing, which again highlights the need to engage with participants more effectively.

Task 10

- Consider how you have developed your own skill set in EAP assessment. What training have you experienced that has informed your practice and to what extent have you learnt on the job?
- Did the qualifications which you have obtained incorporate an element on the topic of assessment? If so, how comprehensive, relevant or useful has this been in your own EAP working context?

Extension activities

The following extension activities can be exploited by colleagues who have additional time to explore and develop the strategies and principles introduced in this chapter.

» Identify an area within your own EAP assessment that you would like to explore further. Use the cycle in Figure 2 to help you to outline what you hope to explore.

» Consider the framework provided in Table 1, which can provide additional structure to the possible research project into EAP assessment which you have identified above.

   » What is the context of your research?

   » What are your research objectives?

   » What would your research questions be?

   » Which hypothesis might you seek to support or refute?

» Plan an assessment-focused collaborative activity which involves working with colleagues from other academic fields that you feel might inform your own EAP assessment. Consider the modules or courses that you are teaching, the needs of your students and any gaps in your knowledge regarding how EAP is used in the target domains in which your other academic colleagues work.

» As colleagues at other institutions are very likely experiencing similar challenges to you, why not instigate a collaborative research project, however big or small, that involves working jointly on an aspect of EAP assessment or which shares good practice in a particular area?

» If you haven't already had the opportunity to do this, why not introduce EAP assessment into a departmental discussion forum, as a means of stimulating colleagues' interest? Try to make the resources that you focus on as accessible as possible by concentrating on what is relevant to your own working context. If you are able to gain the support of another colleague, it could help in the process of understanding and describing the relevance of any more technical resources that you present.

Stakeholder support – 'Did you know …?'

Once you have applied the strategies and principles in this chapter to your EAP assessment context, the following information can be photocopied or adapted for use with different stakeholder groups, such as test takers, parents and staff, who are involved in or affected by your EAP testing and assessment. Consider how this passage could be modified or applied in your own working context.

PHOTOCOPIABLE

Did you know … that we consider collaboration with other EAP and subject-teaching colleagues to be crucial in the process of researching and planning how to teach and assess EAP?

Our EAP practitioners have expertise in teaching and assessing EAP to students who are working towards or within a wide range of academic disciplines. As with other areas of academic investigation and practice, we recognize that this expertise is underpinned by research and collaboration with other experts in the field. In the context of EAP assessment, the expertise that we draw on stems from a range of sources, including:

- EAP-focused scholarly activity
- applied linguistics
- language-teaching pedagogy
- the broader sphere of education

When it comes to understanding the locally focused contexts in which our students are required to use EAP, there are perhaps no better resources than those provided by colleagues and students working and studying in the actual environments or academic domains which our EAP is seeking to target. As a result, some of the most valuable data which are available to us are found in the views of students, teachers and/or lecturers of other academic subjects, who can give us access to their experiences, classrooms and teaching materials. We are then able to use this information to enhance the construct validity of our EAP teaching and assessment.

References

Bachman, L. F. (2000). Modern language testing at the turn of the century: Assuring that what we count counts. *Language Testing, 17*(1), 1–42.

Bool, H., & Luford, P. (1999). *Academic standards and expectations: The role of EAP.* Nottingham: Nottingham University Press.

Brindley, G. (2001). Language assessment and professional development. In C. Elder, A. Brown, K. Hill, N. Iwashita, T. Lumley, T. McNamara, & K. O'Loughlin, (Eds.), *Experimenting with uncertainty: Essays in honour of Alan Davies* (pp. 126–133). Cambridge: Cambridge University Press.

Brown, J. D., & Bailey, K. M. (2008). Language testing courses: What are they in 2007? *Language Testing, 25*(3), 349–383.

Davidson, F., & Lynch, B. K. (2002). *Test craft: A teacher's guide to writing and using language test specifications.* New Haven; London: Yale University Press.

Davies, A. (1990). *Principles of language testing.* Oxford: Basil Blackwell.

Dudley-Evans, T., & St John, M. J. (1998). *Developments in ESP: A multi-disciplinary approach.* Cambridge: Cambridge University Press.

Flowerdew, J., & Peacock, M. (2001). *Research perspectives on English for academic purposes.* Cambridge: Cambridge University Press.

Fulcher, G., & Davidson, F. (2007). *Language testing and assessment: An advanced resource book.* London: Routledge.

Gibbs, G. (1988). *Learning by doing: A guide to teaching and learning methods, Oxford centre for staff and learning development.* London: Further Education Unit.

Hyland, K., & Hamp-Lyons, L. (2002). EAP: Issues and directions. *Journal of English for Academic Purposes, 1*(1), 1–12.

Jafarpur, A. (2003). Is the test constructor a facet? *Language Testing, 20*(1), 57–87.

Manning, A. (2013). *EAP teacher assessment literacy* (Ed.D. thesis). Leicester: University of Leicester.

Popham, W. J. (2009). Assessment literacy for teachers: Faddish or fundamental? *Theory into practice, 48,* 4–11.

Raimes, A. (1991). Out of the woods: Emerging traditions in the teaching of writing. *TESOL Quarterly, 25*(3), 407–430.

Stiggins, R. J. (1991). Assessment literacy. *The Phi Delta Kappan, 72*(7), 534.

Stiggins, R. J. (1995). Assessment literacy for the 21st century. *The Phi Delta Kappan, 77*(3), 238.

Taylor, L. (2009). Developing assessment literacy. *Annual review of Applied Linguistics, 29*, 21–36.

Wallace, M. J. (1991). *Training foreign language teachers: A reflective approach.* Cambridge: Cambridge University Press.

Chapter 7: Marking, grading and the assessment of EAP for learning

This chapter will:
- highlight the importance of a principled approach to marking and scoring.
- introduce and discuss the concept of assessment for learning.

You will have the opportunity to:
- explore some approaches to marking and scoring EAP assessments.
- consider some of the challenges in assessing EAP.
- look at ways to improve your own scoring and grading procedures.

A principled approach to marking and scoring

Marking, grading and the process of giving feedback are key competencies in the process of EAP assessment. Fulcher and Davidson (2007, p. 91) describe the importance of scoring by explaining that the test score is the link between the evidence we elicit from the task on the one hand, and the construct and subject domain on the other.  Fulcher and Davidson (2007, pp. 91–114) also clarify the significance of a principled approach to the process of scoring, given the different nature of reasons and requirements for testing. In some situations, where the objective of testing is predominantly formative in nature, the key objective may be to provide feedback to students, whereas, in other situations, there may be higher stakes where grades are used to draw further inferences or for gate-keeping purposes.

Task 1
- Consider your own EAP assessments and which different situations require different approaches to the scoring and awarding of marks.
- Which of your assessments require particular grades? Has this been affected recently by changes to visa requirements and UK Visas and Immigration (UKVI) policy?

- Which of your assessments are more focused on giving feedback rather than providing scores or grades?
- Do you think that it is possible to undertake summative assessments and successfully provide formative feedback to students at the same time?
- What do you understand by the term 'assessment for learning'?

EAP assessment for learning

'Assessment for learning' positions student assessment at the heart of an integrated approach to student learning and stresses the fact that high quality and appropriate assessment is a prerequisite for better student learning (Knight, 1995).

According to the former Department for Children, Schools and Families (DCSF, 2008): 'Assessment for Learning is an important way of improving students' attainment and is founded on the premise that learners will improve most if they are able to understand the objectives behind their learning, where they are positioned in relation to this objective and how they can achieve the goals which are being targeted'. Consequently, assessment for learning is arguably essential to any effective form of education, where assessment is present or required. Assessment for learning can be defined as the process of seeking and interpreting evidence for use by learners and their teachers to decide where the learners are in their learning, where they need to go and how best to get there (Assessment Reform Group, 2002). As a result, the promotion of assessment for learning and its empowerment for stakeholders, including test takers and teachers who create tests, has certain key shared goals with principled EAP assessment.

Task 2

- Is assessment for learning practised in your own EAP assessment context?
- What is the difference between assessment *of* learning and assessment *for* learning in EAP?
- What sort of practices could be considered to be assessment for learning in EAP?

Popham (2009) highlights the power of assessment for learning when he states that 'when classroom assessments are conceived as assessments for learning, rather than assessments of learning, students will learn better what their teacher wants them to learn' (p. 11).

It is also clear that a number of the features of assessment for learning can be applied directly to the context of principled EAP assessment. This can be seen in Table 1 (adapted from DCSF, 2008 and now adapted to EAP).

Table 2: Features of good assessment for learning, as applied to EAP (adapted from DCSF, 2008)

Feature	Description
An accurate assessment	Knowing what the standards are, judging students' work correctly, and making accurate assessments linked to standards of other programmes or courses which EAP courses are preparing students for.
A fair assessment	Knowing the methods used are valid.
A reliable assessment	Ensuring that judgements are consistent and based on a range of evidence.
A useful assessment	Identifying barriers to student progress and using that information to plan and discuss the next steps in learning.
A focused assessment	Identifying areas of a student's learning where there are blocks to progression, which might, for example, benefit from the attention of additional tuition.
For continuity of assessment	Enabling better transfer between levels and programmes or institutions.

So popular are movements such as assessment for learning that some educational activists, including Black (2003), go as far as to recommend the rejection of emphasis on examination results and reference to league tables in favour of an alternative approach which supports assessment for learning (Biggs & Tang, 2011, p. 64; Knight, 1995).

Task 3

- Consider where you stand on the topic of assessment for learning and the scope you have to implement it in your own EAP assessment context.
- Are you comfortable with the need to assess for institutional purposes or do you feel uncomfortable with the EAP assessment that you are involved with?
- What could you do to improve or change your current situation so that your students are able to learn more from the assessment that they are involved with?
- Do you think it would be possible to move to a position where examination results are no longer considered to be of key importance?

Student-centred approaches which could inform EAP assessment for learning

In the context of modern-day society where examination results continue to play a pivotal role, the requirements of stakeholders may perhaps be better serviced by educationalists such as Gottlieb and Nguyen (2007), who have worked to develop a technique which aims to support the achievement of designated educational outcomes, which may be fixed by national curricular, whilst simultaneously promoting actual progress in transferable learning. Additionally, the work of Price, Rust, O'Donovan and Handley (2012, p. 9) on the topic of Assessment Literacy links in closely with assessment for learning. This is because it maintains that student Assessment Literacy can be considered as a gateway or threshold to further learning as it affords individuals not only the necessary skills and knowledge about assessment good practice, but facilitates the evaluation of educational situations and decision-making regarding which assessment-related skills should be deployed when and for what purpose.

Task 4

- How do you approach the marking of your own EAP assessments?
- Do you use an answer key? If so, how do you decide on which scores should be attributed to which answers? Do you give half marks? Is the awarding of marks consistent? Is the marking information referred to in your test specifications?
- Do you use marking criteria for some of your assessments? If so, how have these criteria been devised? What benchmarks have you referred to in order to build these criteria? Have they been developed for your EAP context?
- Do you or does your department refer to the CEFR?

Attributing scores to performance in EAP assessment

Bachman and Palmer (1996, pp. 51–52) describe two key processes which should be undertaken in order to attribute scores to students' performance in tests or assessments, the first of which includes identifying the number of items which have been successfully answered or completed. This approach involves:

- specifying criteria in order to determine what constitutes successful completion; and
- deciding whether responses will be scored as either correct or incorrect or with varying levels of correctness.

Alternatively, scoring can be undertaken according to levels of language ability. This criterion-based approach involves:

- identifying rating scales in order to assess the language; and

- considering how many stages of ability are to be incorporated into the different scales.

This criterion-based approach links back to outcomes-based planning, as outlined by Fry, Ketteridge and Marshall (2003, pp. 26–41) and as discussed in earlier chapters.

As Hughes (2003, p. 94) explains, the latter approach to scoring can be described as analytic, and commonly involves the award of a separate score for each of a number of aspects of a task, such as lexis, grammar and coherence.

Another existing approach to scoring, known as holistic scoring, is a more impressionistic scoring involving the assignment of a single score based on overall impression. Whilst this approach has the advantage of being very rapid, it makes use of less tangible or scientific reference points and is often based on intuitive shared understandings within teams. It could therefore be challenging to apply in a principled manner in many situations.

A further consideration highlighted by Blue, Milton and Saville (2000, p. 13) relates to different ways in which marking is undertaken across different departments. Blue et al. (ibid., p. 13) make reference to a research project involving both international and home Electrical Engineering students whose written reports were marked by both EAP and Engineering staff using different criteria and returned different results. This collection of articles also makes reference to the predictive validity of test scores obtained by students taking pre-sessional courses in EAP.

Task 5

- Based on some of the details given, consider the marking queries in Figure 1 and identity what the problems may be and how these could be resolved.

- Have you ever encountered situations like this in your own working context? How did you or would you recommend improving the situation?

Just to let you know, I have given half marks for questions 20-25 on the writing paper. I wasn't sure if this was OK, but I felt that it was the right thing to do. I know that not all markers have done the same, but I don't suppose that matters.

Can we possibly meet sometime to talk about the grading criteria for the essay? I can't really see the difference between bands 50-59 and 60-69. One refers to a 'very good' use of grammar and the other to an 'excellent' use of grammar. What's the difference?

For questions 17-19, there are short answer responses and I don't see how the essay grading criteria can be used for these as they're not essay responses. There are five marks for each question. Simon has shared his approach with me. Can I follow that too?

I thought I'd let you know that I showed some of my scripts to Dr Simmonds from Psychology and he was quite surprised about how we interpret the faculty grading criteria in the EAP context. I think you'll be getting an email.

Question 26 requires students to describe a graph. The total mark is out of nine. The marking notes say to mark this question in a similar way to popular external tests which also use a maximum score of nine. Do you have any tips as I haven't marked any of these external tests before?

I know you spent hours putting together the key for the multiple-choice questions last week, but I don't quite agree with some of the correct answers. I think some of the others are just marking exactly according to the key, but when you read some alternative responses some of them don't seem incorrect. What would you recommend?

Figure 1: EAP marking queries

Marking scales

Hughes (2003, pp. 94–100) advises that any scale that is used for scoring should initially be calibrated. This process should involve gathering representative test result samples which represent a model of ability which spans the range of test-taker performance. The assessment team should then examine the samples and award a mark using the scale. This process can then act as a form of training and can also be used as a means of identifying how useful or reliable the scale itself is. In addition to the importance of scale calibration, Hughes stresses the importance of rater training and outlines a three-step training approach.

Task 6

- How have the marking criteria that you use been developed? Has this been a group effort or the work of an individual?
- Have you experienced scale calibration in your own EAP team in advance of using a set of marking criteria?
- What moderation and rater training procedures are practised by the department that you work in? How could these be improved?

Equivalences and the CEFR

In recent years, the ongoing international importance of language testing has been highlighted by the Council of Europe's Common European Framework of Reference for Languages (Council of Europe, 2007). According to the Council of Europe (2003): 'The Common European Framework of Reference for Languages: Learning, teaching, assessment (CEFR) provides a common basis for the elaboration of language syllabuses, curriculum guidelines, examinations, textbooks, etc. across Europe' (p. 13). However, the broad adoption of the CEFR by institutions in Europe and beyond is not without controversy. Weir (2005, p. 282) supports concerns expressed by the Association of Language Testers in Europe (ALTE) when he refers to the possibility of reaching false assumptions of equivalence, if tests which view language constructs in different ways are described using the same terms. This has particular implications for test construct validation. Concern about the use of the CEFR has also reached the mainstream press. North (2004) describes the validation procedures used to develop the CEFR itself. In describing the best way to refer to the CEFR, Fulcher and Davidson (2006) suggest that it should be used to advise the building of context-driven generative test specifications, rather than as a source of final decisions, as it is too general in scope. Fulcher (2004) also describes the dangers of inappropriate application of rating scales through reference to the CEFR.

Stakeholder support – 'Did you know …?'

Once you have applied the strategies and principles in this chapter to your EAP assessment context, the following information can be photocopied or adapted for use with different stakeholder groups, such as test takers, parents and staff, who are involved in or affected by your EAP testing and assessment. Consider how this passage could be modified or applied in your own working context.

PHOTOCOPIABLE

| Did you know … | that we believe in a principled and reliable approach to marking and scoring EAP assessments, given that grades are often used for important admission and progression purposes? |

The EAP assessment team understands that students taking courses and modules in EAP are doing so because they need to maintain or improve their academic English so that they can either demonstrate this for admissions purposes or develop their skills in order to meet the demands of their ongoing studies.

Although we are aware of the importance of attaining particular grades in order to demonstrate achievement of standards or to demonstrate ability, we support assessment for learning which extends far beyond the notion of a single score and can facilitate ongoing learning if it is undertaken effectively.

In the process of marking and scoring EAP tests and assessments, we are familiar with a range of different approaches which can be used in conjunction with different question types.

Our grading criteria and answer keys have been developed with care and attention and have been calibrated with groups of representative markers and raters.

Many of our colleagues are also familiar with external EAP assessment procedures through standardized testing mechanisms, and we understand how this informs our practice and what the limitations of this are in terms of determining equivalences.

Given the importance of the CEFR, we are also aware of how this important resource can interact with other sources of information which can inform language use domain and what the limitations of this are for EAP.

References

Assessment Reform Group. (2002). *Assessment for learning: 10 principles*. Retrieved from http://www.uni-koeln.de/hf/konstrukt/didaktik/benotung/assessment_basis.pdf

Bachman, L. F., & Palmer, A. S. (1996). *Language testing in practice: Designing and developing useful language tests*. Oxford: Oxford University Press.

Biggs, J. B., & Tang, C. S. (2011). *Teaching for quality learning at university: What the student does* (4th ed.). Maidenhead: McGraw-Hill/Society for Research into Higher Education/Open University Press.

Black, P. J. (2003). *Assessment for learning: Putting it into practice*. Maidenhead: Open University Press.

Blue, G. M., Milton, J., & Saville, J. (2000). *Assessing English for academic purposes*. Oxford; New York: P. Lang.

Council of Europe. (2007). *Common european framework of reference for languages: Learning, teaching, assessment (CEFR)*. Retrieved from http://www.coe.int/t/dg4/linguistic/CADRE_EN.asp

Council of Europe. (2009). *Relating language examinations to the common european framework of reference for languages: Learning, teaching, assessment (CEFR)*. Manual. Strasbourg: Council of Europe Language Policy Division.

DCSF. (2008). *The assessment for learning strategy*. Retrieved from https://www.education.gov.uk/publications/eOrderingDownload/DCSF-00341-2008.pdf

Fry, H., Ketteridge, S., & Marshall, S. (2003). *A handbook for teaching and learning in higher education: Enhancing academic practice* (2nd ed.). London: Kogan Page.

Fulcher, G. (2004, March 18). Are Europe's tests being built on an 'unsafe' framework? *The Guardian*. Retrieved from http://www.theguardian.com/education/2004/mar/18/tefl2

Fulcher, G. & Davidson, F. (2006, November 17). Flexibility is proof of a good 'framework'. *The Guardian*. Retrieved from http://www.theguardian.com/education/2006/nov/17/tefl.glennfulcher

Fulcher, G., & Davidson, F. (2007). *Language testing and assessment: An advanced resource book*. London: Routledge.

Gottlieb, M. H., & Nguyen, D. (2007). *Assessment and accountability in language education programs: A guide for administrators and teachers*. Philadelphia, PA: Caslon Pub.

Hughes, A. (2003). Testing English for university study. *ELT Documents* 127. Oxford: Modern English Press.

Knight, P. (1995). *Assessment for learning in higher education*. London: Kogan Page.

North, B. (2004, April 15). Europe's framework promotes language discussion, not directives. *The Guardian*. Retrieved from http://www.theguardian.com/education/2004/apr/15/tefl6

Popham, W. J. (2009). Assessment literacy for teachers: Faddish or fundamental? Theory into practice, 48, 4–11.

Price, M., Rust, C., O'Donovan, B., & Handley, K. (2012). *Assessment literacy: The foundation for improving student learning*. Oxford: Oxford Brookes University.

Weir, C. J. (2005). *Language testing and validation*. Basingstoke: Palgrave Macmillan.

Chapter 8: Text selection, authenticity and specificity

This chapter will:
- introduce you to some key considerations in the process of choosing texts and materials for use in EAP tests.
- provide you with a series of key questions which you can adapt for use in your own context when looking for appropriate texts for EAP tests.

You will have the opportunity to:
- consider the role of authenticity and specificity in texts for use in EAP tests.
- consider available tools which can assist in determining which texts are suitable for use in EAP tests.

Sourcing written or audio/video texts

One common challenge which is experienced by colleagues across the sector, in the process of designing EAP tests, is the identification and selection of texts and materials which are suitable for use in reliable and valid EAP assessments for the purposes of reading or speaking assessments.

Some of the materials which practitioners are likely to consider or encounter include the following types of written or spoken texts:

Table 1: Sources of written or audio/video texts

Sources of written texts	Sources of audio/video texts
Magazine articles	Audio recordings of in-house lectures
Thesis or essay extracts	Video recordings of in-house lectures
Paper-based journal articles	Radio programmes
Online journals	TV programmes
Library books	Podcasts
eBooks	Presentations or lectures shared online
Book chapters	Recorded staged conversations or interviews
Professional or scientific magazines	Recorded staged lecture excerpts
Scholarly search engines	
Academically focused social networks	
Organizational websites	
Online encyclopedias	

Task 1

- How do you usually approach the process of selecting texts for use in EAP tests or assessments?
- Which of the text types in Table 1 do you usually use?
- What are the strengths and weaknesses of using different types of texts?

Challenges presented by different text types

Choosing an appropriate text can be a complex activity which is based on a range of factors, such as the availability of resources, the academic level, the subject focus and the type of EAP test or assessment which is being created. Read the series of EAP rubrics below which have been created for questions connected to reading and audio/visual texts:

1. Read the text below which has been abridged and revised from an article named 'Endangered!' that originally appeared in *Young Geographic* magazine.

2. Before completing this paper, read the literature review on the topic of Value Chain Management. This is taken from a PhD student's recent thesis submission. Once you have read the chapter, answer questions 10–18 and link your answers to what you have learnt this term in your Foundation Business module.

3. Watch the following clip taken from the well-known film, *The Science of Being*. Consider how well this film presents the challenges of studying Science in your experience and how your own goals in studying Science at university relate to the themes in this film.

4. Listen to the following 30-minute excerpt from the radio series, '*Econorama*', which was first aired in May 1996, and answer the following set of ten multiple-choice questions.

5. Review the definitions of five key terms in modern social policy, as described on Wikireader.com, and use this information to assist you in answering questions 10–15. Where possible, support your responses using references to definitions that you have found.

Figure 1: EAP rubrics for written and spoken texts

Task 2

- Through reading the rubrics in Figure 1, what possible problems might arise from the choice of texts in the EAP assessments which are mentioned?
- How could the problems that you have identified be avoided?
- Have you ever experienced any similar issues or problems in the EAP assessments that you have created or experienced in your team?

The role of authenticity

Although authenticity is not usually cited as a critical quality of language testing, Bachman and Palmer (1996, pp. 23–24) argue for an important link between authenticity and construct validity by identifying that authenticity determines the level to which score inferences can be considered representative of the target language use domain. However, it should be noted that Lewkowicz (2000) claims that it is difficult to ascertain the way in which test takers perceive authenticity, and the definition of authenticity may be variable according to different stakeholders.

Bachman and Palmer (ibid., p. 177) clarify that one of the uses of a test specification is to evaluate the relationship or authenticity of tasks in the test, compared to the target language domain.

Authenticity is also referred to as an aspect of identifying test usefulness, an idea which was introduced by Bachman and Palmer (ibid., p. 38) and then revised by Douglas (2000, p. 114). Table 2 summarizes Bachman and Palmer's original model:

Table 2: Characteristics of test usefulness (Bachman & Palmer, 1996, p. 38)

Characteristic	Description
Reliability	Consistency of measurement and avoidance of variation in test scores due to factors other than the construct being measured.
Construct validity	The meaningfulness and appropriateness of the interpretations that we make on the basis of test scores.
Authenticity	The degree of correspondence of the characteristics of a given language test task to the characteristics of a target language use task.
Interactivity	The extent to which the constructs we want to test are critically involved in accompanying the test task.
Impact	The various ways in which the test use affects society.
Practicality	The ways in which the test will be implemented in a given situation, or whether, in fact, the test will be used at all.

Subsequently, Douglas's modification involved the conflation of authenticity and interactiveness into a single dichotomous category. It was felt that in the assessment of language for more specific purposes, such as EAP, there can be no authenticity without the presence of features of the target language use situation, and the interplay with test-takers' knowledge and the test task.

Task 3

- How important is authenticity to you when choosing material to use in EAP tests?
- What constitutes authenticity in your view?
- In what way do you feel authenticity might relate to construct validity?
- How do you select a text to assess either English for General Academic Purposes (EGAP) or English for Specific Academic Purposes (ESAP)?
- What features does a text have to have for use in a specific academic purposes test?

Content validity

Weir (2005), whose research interest aligned with that of Carroll (in Alderson & Hughes, 1981, p. 67) believed that the content validity of assessment material could be achieved in the testing of EAP through analyzing test takers and their needs, and using this information to determine the content of tests. The main means of establishing content validity was through authentic representation of the disciplinary domain (Fulcher & Davidson, 2007, p. 6).

One major criticism of Weir's focus on the communicative situation is that its preoccupation with content, authenticity and sampling does not address the deeper questions about ability and competence, which are now acknowledged as key to construct validity (Fulcher, 1999, p. 223). Furthermore, the difficulty of accurately identifying what constitutes 'authentic situations' was also acknowledged.

Task 4

- In your own context, how do you determine whether your texts and related questions have construct validity, rather than just face validity?
- What procedures do you employ to ensure that a text is relevant to the syllabus taught and is useful in terms of representing the language and skills which students require in their future study contexts?
- Is it possible to compromise on authenticity for the benefit of construct validity, or are the two factors inextricably linked?

Subject knowledge and discipline specificity

With regard to discipline specificity and commercially available tests, Clapham (1996) (and Clapham in Flowerdew & Peacock, 2001, pp. 84–100) discusses the role played by subject knowledge. Clapham's conclusions suggest that a focus on the EGAP common core is the most practical and efficient approach. However, other research for the purposes of TOEFL (Biber, Conrad, Reppen, Byrd, Helt, Clark & Urzua, 2004) remains concerned with the teaching of EAP which is based on the identification of a specific university language register, albeit described on a broader base.

As touched on in Chapter 4 debates surrounding EGAP and ESAP have thrived since the 1970s and '80s (Jordan, 1997; Selinker, Tarone & Hanzeli, 1981; Spack, 1988; Hutchinson & Waters in Swales, 1985; Widdowson, 1983). Seminal articles by Spack (1988) and Dudley-Evans and St John (1998) highlight continuing disputes surrounding what should constitute the domain for EAP and whether there should be emphasis on ESAP or EGAP involving either a subject-specific approach or a focus on a common core of performance, which some believe is shared across academic sub-domains.

Task 5

- What are your views on the assessment for EGAP or ESAP? Which do you think is the most practical? Do your tests tend to be ESAP- or EGAP-focused?

- To what extent is it possible to develop a standard EAP test which accurately reflects the breadth of academic domains?

- How are you able to authentically or specifically represent the academic domains which your EAP assessments are intended to emulate? Which resources could assist you in this process?

- There do now exist a number of course books which attempt to teach ESAP, including a series by the publisher of this book. Should commercial testing organizations consider bringing back the concept of subject-specific modules to cater for different academic domains? Which challenges might these companies face?

Tools for selecting texts for EAP tests

With regard to text selection, Weir (2005, p. 70) clarifies that the purpose of the test will also influence the suitability of any particular text which is chosen for use in the test. For instance, achievement tests may need to draw on material which reflects texts used within the syllabus, whereas proficiency tests may require the sourcing or creation of material which represent a broader subject domain or the type of text used on programmes which students will join after completing EAP courses. The features of writing in particular genres, such as experiment reports for the sciences or critical essays in humanities, should also be taken into account. Alderson (2000) also relates aspects of text choice to the characteristics of successful and unsuccessful readers.

The series of text selection questions, as presented in Table 3, has been compiled in consultation with a range of resources (Weir, 2005; Alderson, 2000; Davies, 2008; Brown & Abeywickrama, 2010; McNamara, 2000; Clapham, 1996). These questions can be used or adapted for the purpose of selecting suitable materials for reading or listening assessment purposes.

Table 3: Text selection questions

Text selection questions	Test creator's comments
Is the text structure clear with coherent argumentation?	
Is the text appropriately organized so that understanding main ideas and gist is feasible?	
Does the text have a suitable level of grammatical cohesion?	
Are at least some of the test takers likely to be able to both understand and respond to the text in the manner you require?	
Is the lexical difficulty of the text appropriate to the level?	
Is the text length appropriate, representative and manageable for the time available?	
Does the text match your expectations using measures such as Flesch–Kincaid, or with reference to academic word lists?	
Is the text genre suitable or appropriate to the academic domain?	

Is the language in the text representative of language constructs which students have been taught and which represent the EAP domain that they are working towards?	
Do the test tasks, which represent the constructs you are assessing, fit appropriately with the text selected?	
Is the text formatting or quality appropriate for the reader or listener?	
How does the text compare to other texts in the assessment? Is it suitably varied in nature, yet equally suitable for the identified purpose?	
Do you feel that the text is appropriate for selection?	
Have you had your decision verified by other colleagues, including representatives from the subject domain?	
Does the text require extensive specific background knowledge?	
Is the text accessible with general knowledge or limited background knowledge?	
Are permissions available to reproduce the text in assessment circumstances?	
Have you modified an original text? Does this in anyway compromise its authenticity or readability in a negative or unrepresentative manner?	

Task 6

- To what extent do you feel that the text selection questions in Table 3 are useful?
- How do you feel they could be enhanced or amended for your own EAP purposes?
- Identify a text that you have used for an EAP listening or reading test and use the text selection questions, or your own modified version, to review the text's suitability. Have you identified any issues which might influence your approach to text selection in future?

A range of online resources now exist which can assist in analyzing the features of written texts. One example of this is a tool which identifies frequently occurring academic vocabulary, as drawn from a particular corpus, when a text is pasted into a search screen. Another example is the analysis of text using assessments of readability, such as Flesch–Kincaid, which evaluates a text and allocates a numerical scale to categorize the text's readability level.

Whilst neither of these tools represent a solution to the complex task of text selection, they provide additional insights which EAP test designers can draw on in the process of their quest.

Task 7

- Identify some of the tools available on the internet which analyze texts using academic word lists or the Flesch–Kincaid readability index. These can be found by typing 'Flesch–Kincaid' or 'Academic word list' into a search engine.

- Look at one of your former EAP tests and select a written text. Paste an excerpt from this text into one of the online tools and consider what the results show in terms of concordance with the academic word lists and the level of readability.

- Consider building in benchmarks to your own test specifications which refer to levels of vocabulary as listed in academic word lists or through Flesch–Kincaid. This could help you to select texts which have similar properties for future test versions.

Remember, however, that professional judgement is still a key factor in text selection, so despite what readability scores might indicate, your views and those of colleagues on a text's suitability are always extremely important.

Extension activities

The following extension activities can be exploited by colleagues who have additional time to explore and develop the strategies and principles introduced in this chapter.

» Adapt one of your EAP test specifications by adding in further details regarding the features of texts which are appropriate for the assessment that you are creating. You could refer to features such as text length, text source or genre, along with other features such as Flesch–Kincaid readability level or frequency of vocabulary for relevant levels within academic word lists.

» Work with at least one other colleague and review a number of versions of one test and compare and contrast the different texts which were used. Try to determine whether the texts are equally fit for purpose or whether some of the texts are better than others. You can then use this information again to define more clearly which texts are appropriate for use in future.

» Consider the extent to which the texts you have selected for assessment purposes are suitably representative of the academic domains that they are intended to reflect. Which features of the text lead you to believe that the text choice is appropriate?

» Consider how you source the materials that you use for either reading or audio/video texts and identify guidelines or recommendations that can provide a consistent and more reliable approach in your department.

» Work as a team to update your departmental policy on the usage of texts and the balance of concern for construct validity, authenticity and face validity. You could then hold a staff CPD session to share this information with colleagues.

Stakeholder support – 'Did you know …?'

Once you have applied the strategies and principles in this chapter to your EAP assessment context, the following information can be photocopied or adapted for use with different stakeholder groups, such as test takers, parents and staff, who are involved in or affected by your EAP testing and assessment. Consider how this passage could be modified or applied in your own working context.

PHOTOCOPIABLE

Did you know … that we take considerable care in identifying appropriate texts to use in the creation of EAP tests and assessments?

The EAP tests and assessments which we create involve the careful identification and selection of reading and audio/video texts. Once these texts have been selected, they are used as stimulus in activities and questions that reflect the key skills that our students need to demonstrate in various academic contexts.

The EAP skills which we seek to measure relate to the EAP skills which our students have acquired through their studies and experience of EAP. As a result, the texts which we use need to accurately represent the academic texts which students will encounter during their particular study contexts.

This means that the features of the texts need not only to appear to be authentic or to seem to be drawn from a relevant field, but that the structure and use of language in the text and the skills which students are required to employ when drawing information from the texts are the same as those which they will need to practise in their academic studies.

References

Alderson, J. C. (2000). *Assessing reading*. Cambridge: Cambridge University Press.

Alderson, J. C., & Hughes, A. (1981). *Issues in language testing*. London: British Council.

Bachman, L. F., & Palmer, A. S. (1996). *Language testing in practice: Designing and developing useful language tests*. Oxford: Oxford University Press.

Biber, D., Conrad, S. M., Reppen, R., Byrd, P., Helt, M., Clark, V., & Urzua, A. (2004). *Representing language use in the university: Analysis of the TOEFL 2000 spoken and written academic language corpus*. ETS TOEFL Monograph Series, MS-25. Princeton, NJ: Educational Testing Service.

Brown, H. D., & Abeywickrama, P. (2010). *Language assessment: Principles and classroom practices*. White Plains, NY: Pearson/Longman.

Carroll, B. J. (1981). Specifications for an English language testing service. In J. C. Alderson & A. Hughes (Eds.), *Issues in language testing*. Oxford: Pergamon Press.

Clapham, C. (1996). *The development of IELTS: A study of the effect of background knowledge on reading comprehension*. Cambridge: Cambridge University Press.

Davies, A. (2008). Textbook trends in teaching language testing. *Language Testing, 25*(3), 327–347.

Douglas, D. (2000), *Assessing languages for specific purposes*. Cambridge: Cambridge University Press.

Dudley-Evans, T., & St John, M. J. (1998). *Developments in ESP: A multi-disciplinary approach*. Cambridge: Cambridge University Press.

Flowerdew, J., & Peacock, M. (2001). *Research perspectives on English for academic purposes*. Cambridge: Cambridge University Press.

Fulcher, G. (1999). Assessment in English for academic purposes: Putting content validity in its place, *Applied Linguistics, 20*(2), 221–236.

Fulcher, G., & Davidson, F. (2007). *Language testing and assessment: An advanced resource book*. London: Routledge.

Hutchinson, T., & Waters, A. (1980). ESP at the crossroads, English for specific purposes, 36. Oregon State University. In J. C. Alderson & A. Hughes (Eds.), *Issues in language testing*. Oxford: Pergamon Press.

Jordan, R. R. (1997). *English for academic purposes: A guide and resource book for teachers*. Cambridge: Cambridge University Press.

Lewkowicz, J. A. (2000). Authenticity in language testing: Some outstanding questions. *Language Testing, 17*(1), 385–402.

McNamara, T. F. (2000). *Language testing.* Oxford: Oxford University Press.

Munby, J. (1978). *Communicative syllabus design: A sociolinguistic model for defining the content of purpose-specific language programmes.* Cambridge: Cambridge University Press.

Selinker, L., Tarone, E., & Hanzeli, V. E. (1981). *English for academic and technical purposes: Studies in honor of Louis Trimble.* Rowley, Massachusetts: Newbury House.

Spack, R. (1988). Initiating ESL students into academic discourse community: How far should we go? *TESOL Quarterly, 22*(1), 29–52.

Swales, J. (1985). *Episodes in ESP: A source and reference book on the development of English for science and technology.* Oxford: Pergamon Institute of English.

Weir, C. J. (2005). *Language testing and validation: An evidence-based approach.* Basingstoke: Palgrave Macmillan.

Widdowson, F. (1983). *Going up into the next class: Women and elementary teacher training 1840–1914.* London: Hutchinson.

Chapter 9: Understanding statistics and how descriptive procedures can be used to analyze EAP test results

This chapter will:
- explain the importance of using statistics to analyze the results of EAP tests and assessments.
- introduce a number of descriptive statistical procedures which you might find useful in your EAP assessment context.

You will have the opportunity to:
- explore how certain descriptive statistical techniques can be applied to your own EAP assessment context.

In many cases, the skills honed by EAP teachers are different to those of the statistician. Indeed, some language teaching professionals may even have chosen their career to avoid the scientific disciplines (Bachman, 2004, p. ix).

Nevertheless, given the close association of high-stakes testing with measurement and aspirations of precision, it is necessary for the repertoire of EAP assessors' skills to involve development of at least some skills in using statistics.

Task 1

- What is your experience of using statistics in the process of interpreting the results of EAP tests that your students have taken?
- Do you agree or disagree with the idea that statistics are useful in the process of understanding and evaluating test results?
- Would you say that you are comfortable or uncomfortable with using statistics?
- Which statistical procedures have you become used to using during your career?

- What kind of additional support or assistance would you benefit from?
- If you use an internet search engine or an online video website, you can find a lot of support resources to assist with understanding and using a range of statistical procedures. The examples used in this media are often more straightforward than statistics textbooks, which don't always cater for the needs of less experienced users of statistics.

Key works which are relevant and accessible to contemporary EAP practitioners are produced by experts in this field, such as Bachman (2004), Bachman and Kunnan (2005) and Larson-Hall (2010). These resources offer an invaluable transferable toolkit for the purpose of applying statistical procedures specifically to language-testing situations relevant to EAP; they also provide electronic resources linked to software packages such as SPSS and Excel, so that users can put theory into practice.

Task 2

- Which resources have you drawn on to inform any use of statistics in your analysis of EAP test results?
- If you have drawn on any resources, how did you find these resources in terms of usability?
- How do you identify which statistics to use for particular purposes?
- Have you had any formal training in how to use statistics in the interpretation of EAP test results?
- Is there any training that you would like? Do you have any colleagues who could assist?

The benefits of the use of statistics can be described in terms of the manner in which they facilitate analysis of complex numerical data and the identification of trends (Woods, Fletcher & Hughes, 1986, p. 1). In addition, in line with a multidimensional view of validity (Messick, 1989, p. 20), Gorard (2001, p. 5) states that qualitative investigations which are completed without any concern for quantitative support risk compromising the value of interpretations which are gleaned.

Arguably one of the most difficult choices presented to lay statisticians involves identifying the most appropriate statistical analysis tools to use (Brown, 1988, p. 113), as reliance on the incorrect technique will produce inaccurate or misleading results.

Task 3

- How familiar are you with the use of descriptive statistics?
- Do you know how descriptive statistics differ from inferential statistics?
- Are you familiar with how to use software packages to interpret or evaluate test data?
- What, in your view, are some of the main applications for statistics in the EAP assessment process?

Descriptive statistics are useful for identifying groupings or distributions within a set of data.

Objectives 1A–1C that follow present and explain some of the objectives and features of descriptive statistical procedures which are described in a number of the key EAP assessment texts which advocate the use of statistics. These procedures should be considered by EAP practitioners seeking to develop this aspect of skill or repertoire in EAP assessment. In summary, methods suggested in Objectives 1A–1C can be used for purposes such as to:

- investigate and display the distribution of marks within a set of test scores to see how grades in a test are spread.

- consider how grades are grouped and to identify average or central tendencies within a group of scores.

- examine the variability of distribution of test scores and the difference between the highest and lowest scores from a test.

Task 4

- Review the list of purposes to which statistical procedures can be applied and consider your own experience.
- If you have not yet attempted to use statistics in one of the listed ways, which could you try?
- Which procedures are considered to be more powerful?
- Are there any suggestions listed which appear daunting to you that you could source help or support for?

Table 1, based on Brown (1988, pp. 20–23), presents a common range of quantitative measurement scales and examples which characterize their usage in an EAP context. Through understanding the nature of the data collected, along with its features and inherent categories, this can assist in the process of identifying appropriate methods for analysis.

Table 1: Measurement scales (based on Brown, 1988, pp. 20–23)

Scale type	Features	Example	Calculating central tendency/ distribution
Nominal	Provides names and categories only (no order implied).	Dichotomous: Gender: Male and female Non-dichotomous: Nationality: British, American, Korean. This could be useful when investigating the characteristics of an EAP class.	Mode only
Ordinal	Provides categories, but also provides the ordering or ranking of those categories (no information about distance between categories).	This could be useful for EAP test items which are dichotomous, such as *True/False* questions. Non-dichotomous ordinal scales include Likert scales which consist of multiple values, such as 'strongly agree', 'agree', 'neither agree nor disagree', 'disagree' and 'strongly disagree'. These are more likely to be used in surveys or opinion polls, so you might encounter them in feedback from your students.	Mode or median / range, interquartile range
Interval	Provides categories and ordering, and shows distance between points in that ordering. Notably, intervals have the same interpretation throughout (no absolute Zero).	For example, if final test scores in an EAP test are reported as grades such as A, B, C, this is an interval scale provided that the increment between each grade is the same, e.g.: A = 81–100 B = 61–80 C = 41–60 D = 21–40 E = 0–20 There is no absolute Zero. For example, the attainment of a score of zero on a language test does not represent the complete absence of language ability.	Mode, median and mean / range, interquartile range / standard deviation
Ratio	Provides the intervals between points in the ordering of certain categories, but with more information because there is an interpretable zero and multiples of points along the scale make sense.	For ratio scales, it is possible to refer to zero or multiples. For example, in the case of electricity, if a 50-watt bulb is turned on and then an additional 100-watt bulb is illuminated, now three times the amount of electricity is being used. If both are turned off, there is zero electricity in use. Ratio scales are not so applicable to the context of EAP because it is difficult to say that a test taker has zero EAP skill or that (s)he is three times as skilled in assessment than another person.	Mode, median, mean or geometric mean (multiplying a set of figures and dividing by the number of figures multiplied, e.g., useful for calculating average rates of growth) / range, interquartile range / standard deviation

Descriptive statistical analysis procedures and resources for EAP language testers (Objectives 1A–1C)

> **Objective 1A:** To investigate the spread or distribution of scores or grades (Bachman, 2004, pp. 41–54; Dörnyei, 2007, p. 208; Larson-Hall, 2010, p. 245).

Distribution is typically used in order to describe the shape and characteristics of a score dispersal, identify outliers or anomalous scores and as a precursor to using descriptive statistics of grouping. Often, scores are arranged or displayed in:

- an ordered list
- tabular form
- frequency polygons

The term normal distribution, often used to describe a frequency polygon, takes the form of a bell curve. Normal distributions, which can vary in shape, appear in many naturally occurring situations, including in educational variables relevant to EAP, such as ability in different language skills.

In a frequency polygon, for the purpose of discussing score dispersal, the term *kurtosis* is used to refer to the level of peakedness in symmetrical distributions. Kurtosis is often described using the following terms:

- leptokurtic – highly peaked
- platykurtic – relatively flat
- mesokurtic – middle peaked (typical of normal distribution)

Skewness (in a frequency polygon) can also be used to refer to distributions which show a form of asymmetry. Skewness is often described as:

- positively skewed – longer tail at upper end and peak at lower end
- negatively skewed – longer tail at lower end and peak at upper end
- bimodal distribution – two peaks

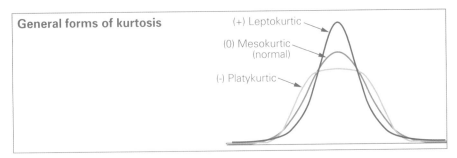

General forms of kurtosis

(+) Leptokurtic

(0) Mesokurtic (normal)

(-) Platykurtic

Biomodal distribution

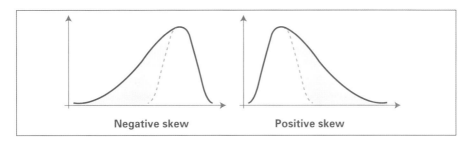

Negative skew   Positive skew

Other means of presentation include:

- histogram/bar chart

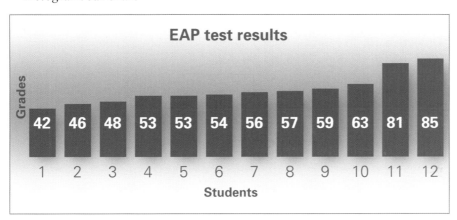

- box-and-whisker plot

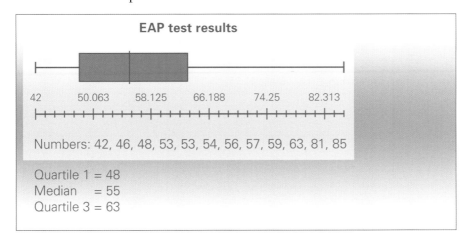

Task 5

- Take a set of data from one of your past tests and experiment by trying to create one or more of the charts suggested. In some cases, you can use normal office-based software for this purpose and, if you need further guidance, online search engines often provide video tutorials to assist. Other procedures may require more specialist software packages. Investigate which software licences are available through your institution and see if you can gain some support through formal training or a colleague.

- Once you have created a chart, examine it and consider what the data shows you. Is your data normally distributed in a form of bell curve? Does the data lean towards the upper level of the scale used to mark your test? Are most grades clustered around the middle portion of your scale, thus creating a platykurtic curve? What do you notice?

- Does this give you any additional insight into your tests, their results or your marking procedures?

Objective 1B: To examine how grades or scores are grouped (Bachman, 2004, pp. 55–62; Kirk, 2008, pp. 68–73).

Descriptive statistics of grouping are indicators of central tendency, often expressed as a number or percentage, and displayed individually or collectively in tabular form, or marked on a frequency polygon.

Mode

The mode (the most frequently occurring score) of different groups is useful for describing demographic information, such as age, sex and level of education, to understand characteristics of test takers.

Group 1   Q1   Q2   Q3

42	46	48	53	53	54	56	57	59	63	81	85

For the data for Group 1, the mode is 53.

Median

The median is the midpoint value in a series of data and splits the data into two equal sets. The median can also be expressed as the same figures as the second quartile (Q2). This is a point in the distribution above which exactly half of the scores occur and below which the other half occur.

For the data for Group 1, the median is 55.

Mean

The mean, or the average of a test score, is often interpreted as an indicator of test difficulty or how a given group of students has performed. It is calculated as the sum of the scores gained on the test, divided by the number of test takers to which the scores pertain.

For the data for Group 1, the mean is 58.

Objective 1C: To describe the variability or distribution of test scores (Bachman, 2004, pp. 63–67; Kirk, 2008, p. 106).

Range

The range shows the difference between the highest and lowest scores. It can be calculated by subtracting the lowest score from the highest score. It does, however, include extreme values which can skew perceptions of dispersion. The range can be expressed as an interval such as 5–75 (5 = lowest and 75 = highest) or an interval width such as 70 (for the range above).

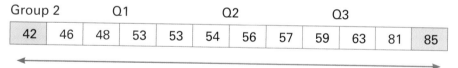

Group 2 | Q1 | Q2 | Q3

| 42 | 46 | 48 | 53 | 53 | 54 | 56 | 57 | 59 | 63 | 81 | 85 |

For the data for Group 2, the range is 43.

Interquartile range

The interquartile range is the range of the central half of a set of data. When compared to the range, the interquartile range is a more effective measure of central tendency, as it focuses on the spread of the middle half of the values. It is based on the principle that, for any symmetrical (not skewed) distribution, half of its values will be found in one semi-interquartile range either side of the median (Q2). If the data set contains outliers, the range alone can appear very large. However, it will not represent the data properly. In contrast, the interquartile range is not influenced by outlying data. The interquartile range is highlighted below:

Group 3			Q1			Q2			Q3		
42	46	48	53	53	54	56	57	59	63	81	85

For the data for Group 3, the interquartile range is 6.

Semi-interquartile range/quartile deviation

The semi-interquartile range is the interquartile range divided by two (Q3–Q1) ÷ 2. It is a measure of variability which is frequently used for data sets which are not normally distributed. As the semi-interquartile range spans one half the distance between Q1 and Q3, it is even less affected by extreme scores than the interquartile range. When data distribution is very skewed and normally distributed, it is more useful to use the semi-interquartile range to describe dispersion along with the median.

For the data above, the semi-interquartile range is 3.

Standard deviation

The standard deviation shows how much, on average, test scores vary or deviate from the mean. In a situation where there is a form of normal distribution, if cases are fairly tightly clustered together and the bell-shaped curve is steep, the standard deviation is small. When the examples are distributed further apart and there is a flatter bell curve, there will be a comparably larger standard deviation.

For the data above, the standard deviation is 13.

Task 6

- Look again at the descriptive statistics, consider creating a descriptive statistical report based on each of your sets of EAP test results.
- Take a data set from a previous EAP assessment and work out the mode, median, mean, standard deviation and range. You could make this a standard feature of reporting your EAP test results which could be used to compare the features of different cohorts in different terms or academic years.

Extension activities

The following extension activities can be exploited by colleagues who have additional time to explore and develop the strategies and principles introduced in this chapter.

» Try to create a frequency polygon which shows the distribution of grades in a set of marks from one of your EAP tests. To turn your set of results into a frequency polygon, remember that the X-axis is used to represent the different marks gained by the students who completed your EAP test. The Y-axis shows the frequency or the number of times that each score was obtained. Perhaps the easiest way to create the polygon is to first create a histogram with a bar to represent the frequency that each EAP score was obtained. You can do this in most spreadsheet software packages. The polygon is then created by marking the upper central element of each bar and effectively joining the dots. You can also do this in the same spreadsheet software. When you have completed the polygon, consider what the pattern reveals about the distribution of grades.

» A number of websites exist which offer online calculators to assist with descriptive statistical procedures. Try using a search engine and typing keywords such as 'Mean calculator' or 'Box and whisker calculator'. Once you have identified a useful online calculator, take some data from one of your past EAP tests and see if you can use the calculator to perform one of the procedures.

» Look at the support materials that you use to report the results of your tests and assessments to students, staff or members of the public. Consider adding a chart which presents some statistical information relating to your test scores.

» Once you have decided which statistical procedures might be useful for your own tests and working context, consider referring to these in the test specification, so that you remember to run the procedures after each sitting of a test or assessment, where relevant.

Stakeholder support – 'Did you know ...?'

Once you have applied the strategies and principles in this chapter to your EAP assessment context, the following information can be photocopied or adapted for use with different stakeholder groups, such as test takers, parents and staff, who are involved in or affected by your EAP testing and assessment. Consider how this passage could be modified or applied in your own working context.

PHOTOCOPIABLE

Did you know ... that we understand the importance of using descriptive statistics to reveal meanings in our EAP test results?

Assessment and testing in EAP can have important repercussions for admission onto courses and the attainment of qualifications, which can affect people's lives. As a result, it is important that the scrutiny and investigation of EAP test scores involves more than just qualitative analysis. If statistical procedures are used appropriately, the broader meaning expressed by a set of results can be appreciated and acted upon more easily and usefully.

- The application of descriptive statistics can be seen in a range of situations in the EAP context. These include processes such as:
- frequency polygons or histograms to explore distributions of grades
- the mean, mode and median scores
- calculating the range
- identifying the standard deviation

The use of descriptive statistics is common to identify groupings in a set of EAP results and these processes can be very revealing in terms of the spread of grades and the patterns of results which are revealed across a class or particular cohort of students.

Through using a range of statistical procedures in our analysis of EAP test results, we aim to communicate results of tests and their meanings to our stakeholders. It is our hope that this is achieved in a way which allows people to interpret the results of EAP tests more accurately and efficiently.

References

Bachman, L. F. (2004). *Statistical analyses for language assessment*. Cambridge: Cambridge University Press.

Bachman, L. F., & Kunnan, A. J. (2005). *Statistical analyses for language assessment: Workbook and CD-ROM*. Cambridge: Cambridge University Press.

Brown, J. D. (1988). *Understanding research in second language learning: A teacher's guide to statistics and research design*. Cambridge: Cambridge University Press.

Dörnyei, Z. (2007). *Research methods in applied linguistics: Quantitative, qualitative, and mixed methodologies*. Oxford: Oxford University Press.

Gorard, S. (2001). *Quantitative methods in educational research: The role of numbers made easy*. London: Continuum.

Kirk, R. E. (2008). *Statistics: An introduction* (5th ed.). Belmont: Thomson Wadsworth.

Larson-Hall, J. (2010). *A guide to doing statistics in second language research using SPSS*. London: Routledge.

Messick, S. (1989). Validity. In R. L. Linn (Ed.), *Educational measurement* (3rd ed., p. 610). New York: American Council on Education.

Woods, A., Fletcher, P., & Hughes, A. (1986). *Statistics in language studies*. Cambridge: Cambridge University Press.

Chapter 10: Inferential statistics and applications in EAP assessment

This chapter will:
- illustrate how inferential statistics can be used in the analysis of EAP tests and their results.
- present a series of inferential statistical procedures which can be applied to your own EAP assessment context.

You will have the opportunity to:
- explore a broader range of meanings from the results and test scores that emerge from your EAP assessments.

Inferential statistics are usually believed to be more useful in terms of generalization than descriptive alternatives (Gorard, 2001, p. 150); this is because they provide a better gauge of how the analysis of a sample may relate to larger groups of people (Brown, 1988, p. 115). Such data enables a step beyond descriptive analysis of the particular sample collected, by generalizing findings to the wider population (Dörnyei, 2007, p. 115; Larson-Hall, 2010, p. 45).

In summary, methods suggested in Objectives 1A–1D can be used to:

- reveal relationships between different variables, such as different sections within a test.

- explore reliability or difficulty of test items so that unreliable or ineffective items can be discarded and revised.

- assess the reliability of item sets, sections or test versions or the reliability of raters.

- inspect the validity of constructs within tests.

Inferential statistical analysis procedures and resources for EAP (Objectives 1A–1D)

> **Objective 1A:** To investigate relationships between two different entities (Bachman, 2004, pp. 80–85; Dörnyei, 2007, pp. 223–225; Gorard, 2001, pp. 167–170).

Correlation coefficients are statistics calculated from data which summarize the strength and direction of the relationship between two variables. Correlation coefficients range between negative one (-1.00) and positive one (+1.00). Positive coefficients indicate direct relationships, while negative coefficients indicate inverse relationships. The larger the coefficient, positive or negative, the stronger the relationship. A correlation near to zero suggests a weak relationship and a correlation near to one (either positive or negative) shows a strong relationship. In EAP, this kind of procedure could be used to calculate the correlation between students' results in, for example, separate reading and writing tests to ascertain whether there is a correlation between high or low grades in reading and high or low grades in writing.

Pearson product-moment correlation coefficient

This technique requires the relationship between the two variables to be linear; both variables should constitute interval scales and both should be normally distributed. For example, the data below were collected from the results obtained by 28 students, each of whom completed two 50-item tests, one test focusing on academic vocabulary and the other on broader academic reading skills. In each case, the maximum score was 50.

Student	S1	S2	S3	S4	S5	S6	S7	S8	S9	S10	S11	S12	S13	S14
Vocab	8	9	15	16	17	19	21	21	21	22	23	24	25	26
Reading	9	7	17	15	18	18	20	19	22	24	46	25	26	25

Student	S15	S16	S17	S18	S19	S20	S21	S22	S23	S24	S25	S26	S27	S28
Vocab	26	27	28	29	29	29	30	31	35	36	39	41	43	44
Reading	25	26	30	27	29	28	31	30	32	35	37	40	42	46

As the scatter diagram shows, there is a discernible correlation in the spread of grades indicated by the visible line. An outlier is notable in the value 46, which does not follow the pattern or direction of the score from the other test taken by the same student. This is caused by a student gaining 23/50 in the vocabulary test and 46/50 in the reading test. There may be an explanation for this which is worthy of investigation.

In this case, the results show that the value of 'r' is 0.8927. The Pearson correlation coefficient, referred to as 'r', can be anything from +1 to -1. An 'r' value of 0 shows that there is no correlation between the two listed variables. Values which are greater than 0 indicate a positive correlation. This 'r' shows a strong positive correlation, which means that high X (vocabulary test) variable scores go with high Y (reading test) variable scores (and vice versa).

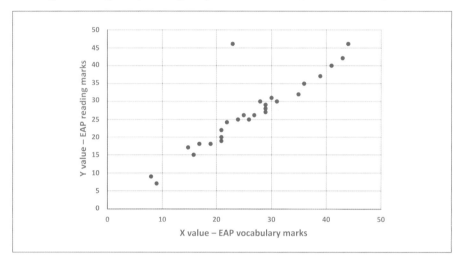

Other correlation procedures also exist, such as Spearman Rank Correlation, which can be used to investigate the relationship between two variables without interval measures or normal distribution.

Task 1

- Take a set of results from one of your previous EAP test papers and see if you can use some of the results to identify any relationships between different test papers or sets of results. See if the information and the correlations which are revealed match your expectations or if they tell you something about your teaching or students' learning processes.

- If you aren't able to use past sets of data, consider reviewing the way you arrange your questions and design your tests so that you might be able to investigate correlations in the future. Remember, you should only do this if it doesn't adversely affect the validity or integrity of your EAP tests.

Item difficulty statistics

Statistics such as the Item difficulty index, Item discrimination index and Item-total test score correlations can be used to:

- give feedback to test takers, teachers and test developers.
- help identify problems with items which can help with control characteristics of score distribution.
- identify weaknesses for correction, to increase the internal consistency and reliability of a test.
- ascertain why items are not operating satisfactorily.

As an example, in order to calculate how difficult a particular set of EAP test questions is, the difficulty index can be determined. In the case of multiple-choice questions, this procedure requires EAP assessors to work out the number of test takers who provided the correct response. It is also possible to identify faulty items by looking at the number of instances of selection of the range of alternatives provided. The data below show the responses to an EAP cloze vocabulary activity with five options (A, B, C, D and E), where 42 took the test.

Item	A	B	C	D	E
1	5	0	29*	3	5
2	11	20*	5	4	2

* correct answer

In the case of the first item, it is clear that option B did not function well as a distractor, as no test takers chose this option. The difficulty index is calculated by dividing the number of test takers who chose the correct answer – in this case, option C, with 29 responses – by the total number of people who took the test, 42. Using this approach, the difficulty of Item 1 is 29/42, which equals 69. In general, if the difficulty is calculated as 75 or more, then it can be considered to be an easy item, and if a value of 25 or less is returned, it may be considered hard. In this situation, whilst 69 is not yet in the easy band, it is quite close, so it may be suitable to consider modifying the distractors used in A, B, D and E, so that the question challenges a wider spread of test takers. On the other hand, for Item 2, correct responses to B total 20, which results in a difficulty of 47. This item could be considered to be more difficult.

Task 2

- Look back at a bank of multiple-choice questions that you have used in the past in an EAP assessment and calculate the Item difficulty index.

- Consider which questions appear to be too difficult or too hard and which distractors may be underperforming. What changes can you make to improve your questions and avoid overly easy or difficult items?

Objective 1C: To test hypotheses between different groups or variables; to investigate internal reliability of test scores; to test reliability of grading procedures (Bachman, 2004, pp. 159–174; Dörnyei, 2007, pp. 215–219; Fulcher & Davidson, 2007, p. 105; Larson-Hall, 2010, pp. 241–243, pp. 268–269).

The procedures below are used to compare the scores of different groups who have taken the same test or the scores from a single group that has taken different tests.

T-tests and ANOVA

A number of procedures are used to identify differences between two or more different groups of test score or class performance, based on different variables, such as teaching methodology.

A T-test is typically used to compare the results for two groups.

An ANOVA (analysis of variance) is employed for more than two groups. These analyses can help answer questions such as: If the level or quality of one variable is modified, then will this also affect the level of the other variable? In the case of EAP, the variables could relate to a particular teaching or assessment technique or method.

Independent (unmatched) sample T-tests can be used where it is necessary to compare the scores of groups or classes that are independent of each other. For example, Class A and Class B.

Paired-sample T-tests are used in circumstances where it is necessary to compare two sets of scores (two variables) collected from the same group or class, for example, EAP Class A's scores on two different tests. This type of

T-test is also used when the same individuals are tested more than once, such as via a pre-course test and a post-course test.

The following example is the result of a paired sample T-test, which is used to compare two sets of EAP scores that are related to each other. In this case, it compares the results of two EAP speaking tests given to the same class. Although the total score for both EAP speaking tests is 55, different kinds of prompt card are used in each of the two interview tests. The procedure can be used to ascertain if students' responses are significantly different based on the use of alternative prompt cards in the two EAP speaking tests.

The data sets below represent the results from speaking test 1 (ST1) and 2 (ST2), given to the same class.

Student	S1	S2	S3	S4	S5	S6	S7	S8	S9	S10	S11	S12	S13	S14
ST1	11	18	19	20	23	25	25	25	26	28	29	30	31	31
ST2	8	20	18	22	22	24	23	26	29	55	30	31	30	30

Student	S15	S16	S17	S18	S19	S20	S21	S22	S23	S24	S25	S26	S27
ST1	32	34	35	35	35	36	37	42	43	47	49	52	53
ST2	31	36	32	35	34	37	36	38	42	44	48	50	55

After completing the T-test calculation, the value of 't' is returned as 0.551761. The value of 'p' is 0.585651.

In statistics, the t-value indicates the size of an effect, from the perspective of a bell curve, which shows probability distribution. The greater the distance of the t-value from 0, the more probable that the effect is of statistical significance and therefore produced via a repeatable cause, rather than random chance. In this particular context 0.551761 is not greatly higher than 0 and therefore does not strongly support any effect from the use of the prompt cards.

The p-value is an additional tool which estimates the probability of rejecting the null hypothesis. In other words, the p-value can also be seen as the likelihood of finding the same or higher results when the null hypothesis is supported. The null hypothesis in this case can be described as '*no difference in student responses based on response card*'. Consequently, it can be considered that the result is not significant at $p \leq 0.05$.

When the t- and p-values are considered in tandem, again this infers that the use of the different prompt cards has not had a significant impact on test results.

Measures of internal reliability or consistency

Other procedures, listed below, can be used to examine internal consistency within a test and reliability of items and sections:

- Split half estimates (Guttman/Spearman-Brown) Norm Referenced (NR)
  - Test takers' results on a test are split into two halves to examine reliability across two parallel sets.
- Estimates based on item variances (Cronbach's Alpha) (NR)
  - The scores obtained on individual parallel test items are examined for variance.
- Test-retest reliability estimates (also known as stability tests) (NR)
  - Give the same test to the same group of test takers twice, with a time delay between administrations, and to analyze the variance in results.

As an example, Cronbach's Alpha can be used to gauge the internal reliability of items which have been designed to measure the same EAP construct (Dörnyei, 2007, pp. 206–207). If an EAP test has been devised to measure understanding or usage of particular connective devices, then Cronbach's Alpha could be employed to identify whether, in most cases, respondents who identified 'Consequently' as the correct option in Question A, also identified 'Consequently' as correct in the three other items where this connective device is also the correct answer. This type of correlation indicates a reliable representation of a construct in a test. However, if in response to questions where 'Consequently' is the correct response, respondents gave notably divergent ratings, this absence of correlation may suggest that the items do not measure the same construct and, therefore, that those items should be removed or rephrased.

Additional procedures listed below are used to investigate reliability of procedures associated with marking and awarding grades:

- Rater (Marker) reliability estimates (NR)
  - This can be used to determine EAP inter-rater or intra-rater reliability.
- Phi coefficient dependability Criterion Referenced (CR)
  - This procedure can be used to measure the dependability of an EAP test score as a measure of mastery in a skill.
- Agreement indices
  - These are used to measure reliability of different classifications or bands related to mastery or non-mastery of EAP skills.

Task 3

- Collect some data from the results of your past EAP tests with a view to undertaking a T-test. Try a paired-sample T-test to compare two sets of scores collected from the same group. For example, you could compare the results drawn from two writing activities drawn from Task A and Task B in a single EAP writing paper.

- When you have completed the T-test, what have you noticed in terms of the significance of the differences in the values which have been returned? Do the results suggest that the EAP test takers perform similarly on both tasks, or are the results divergent?

- If difference in the results is statistically significant, is this explainable and acceptable, or will you need to modify your test and its specification?

Objective 1D: To investigate test validity (Bachman, 2004, pp. 257–293; Fulcher & Davidson, 2007, p. 184).

The following techniques could be considered by EAP test developers as a mechanism to explore test validity.

Use of expert raters

In this process, raters are skilled practitioners in EAP, whose expert judgement is used to quantify the suitability of test content, often using rating scales. Typically, raters can be asked to annotate EAP tests or test items. A score can be awarded to indicate raters' views on the suitability or validity of different items.

Verbal protocols

This technique involves the analysis of test-taker experiences, which are given verbally after a test has been taken. Content analysis can be employed in order to identify patterns or themes in a series of transcribed comments, as provided by test takers.

Task 4

- Identify a reliable colleague or group of colleagues and ask them to review one of your EAP tests or test specifications. You could devise a scale which will allow them to identify the extent to which they feel that each of your items is an appropriate or valid measure of the constructs which you are trying to measure. Once your colleagues have reviewed and annotated your test papers, consider any patterns which might indicate the need to revise your items in order to enhance validity.

- Invite a group of test takers to be interviewed shortly after the completion of an EAP test and ask them a series of questions about their experience of the EAP test and any problems that they encountered or suggestions that they might have for enhancement. Once the data has been collected, and if possible transcribed, try to identify patterns of theme which can be considered when revising or enhancing your tests and preparatory materials.

Exploratory factor analysis

This procedure can involve analysis of patterns in test scores of test takers who have taken a number of different test versions. Factor analysis can be used to examine the construct validity of items through the process of reducing or clustering a larger number of variables in the form of responses to different test items to a smaller number (Bachman, 2004, pp. 257–293; Fulcher & Davidson, 2007, p. 184). In brief, this allows responses to similar items which test the same construct to be conflated as a more powerful measure.

Rasch Analysis

This statistical procedure can be used by EAP test developers who intend to use the total score on a test or questionnaire to summarize each person.

A Rasch Analysis offers evidence with regard to:

- the extent to which a particular EAP item may under- or over-discriminate in relation to the overall total test score.

- two or more groups in which any EAP test item may function differently.

- variances with regard to the statistical independence of the items.

Through consideration and further exploration of the resources above, the EAP practitioner can become familiar with a means of providing quantitative evidence in order to support test use (Bachman, 2004, p. x). Given the high-stakes nature of EAP, this aspect of assessment skill is crucial as it assists in enabling us to demonstrate whether or not tests are reliable and, therefore, can be used to mitigate the risk associated with unfair decision-making and the impact which this can have on individuals.

Task 5

- If you are able to access a specialist statistics software package, try to analyze a bank of related multiple-choice questions using factor analysis. This process enables a more scientific identification of which sub-items actually group to form factors or constructs and which items did not group as you might have expected.

- If you are able to undertake a factor analysis and you do identify some items which don't seem to measure the target construct as you intended, are you able to identify why and to rephrase the question for future, more effective use?

Extension activities

The following extension activities can be exploited by colleagues who have additional time to explore and develop the strategies and principles introduced in this chapter.

» Work together with a colleague and try to practise using inferential statistics to calculate correlations relating to the results obtained by a class of students who have completed both a reading and a writing test. Do the results show a correlation between high grades in academic reading and high grades in academic writing?

» Experiment with a paired sample T-test by comparing two sets of EAP scores that are related to each other. This could be the results of two similar EAP tests or quizzes given to the same class. You might chose a mid-term and an end-of-term test, for example.

» If you use multiple-choice questions in any of your assessments, consider using Cronbach's Alpha to assess the reliability of a bank of questions that you are using to assess a particular construct.

» Use an online video website to find one or more web tutorials related to inferential statistical procedures that you aren't yet familiar with. Try to use the video to help you to understand how to use one of the procedures suggested in this chapter.

» If you teach on an international course which includes subject modules, ask a teacher who has experience with statistics to assist you with some of the procedures that you may be interested in calculating. You might find that teachers who work in the field of Mathematics or Psychology have some key skills in the use of statistics that could be useful as part of your own training.

Stakeholder support – 'Did you know …?'

Once you have applied the strategies and principles in this chapter to your EAP assessment context, the following information can be photocopied or adapted for use with different stakeholder groups, such as test takers, parents and staff, who are involved in or affected by your EAP testing and assessment. Consider how this passage could be modified or applied in your own working context.

Did you know … that we use inferential statistics in the analysis of our EAP tests and their results in order to reveal deeper meanings and relationships between data?

Language teachers may not always be familiar with procedures which extend beyond descriptive statistics. However, we believe that the use of more complex inferential statistical procedures can help us as EAP practitioners to delve beneath surface-level interpretations of data sets and to make generalizations which relate to broader circumstances and populations.

It is commonly accepted that inferential statistics are believed to be more powerful that descriptive statistics, as inferential statistics provide a better indication of how results relate to larger groups of people. Examples of how inferential statistics can be applied to a range of different situations in EAP test analysis include investigations of:

- reliability of item sets and/or raters
- relationships and correlations between results from different test sections
- validity of test constructs

Through the use of inferential statistics, information can be gleaned relating to test scores which can show interactions, patterns or trends, which, under the right conditions, can be used to demonstrate broader impacts, or which can also be used to demonstrate the need to adapt tests in order to improve their reliability or validity as testing tools.

References

Bachman, L. F. (2004). *Statistical analyses for language assessment.* Cambridge: Cambridge University Press.

Brown, J. D. (1988). *Understanding research in second language learning: A teacher's guide to statistics and research design.* Cambridge: Cambridge University Press.

Dörnyei, Z. (2007). *Research methods in applied linguistics: Quantitative, qualitative, and mixed methodologies.* Oxford: Oxford University Press.

Fulcher, G., & Davidson, F. (2007). *Language testing and assessment: An advanced resource book.* London: Routledge.

Gorard, S. (2001). *Quantitative methods in educational research: The role of numbers made easy.* London: Continuum.

Larson-Hall, J. (2010). *A guide to doing statistics in second language research using SPSS.* London: Routledge.

Chapter 11: Washback

This chapter will:
- describe a number of key issues associated with washback in EAP assessment.
- introduce a range of implications and context whereby washback can have negative implications for EAP skill acquisition.

You will have the opportunity to:
- reflect on your own experiences of washback in EAP assessment and what can be learnt from these situations.
- consider ways in which washback can be avoided in EAP assessment.
- review the impact of washback from standardized EAP tests and in-house EAP assessment mechanisms.

When the tail wags the dog

One particular phenomenon connected to language testing and high-stakes assessment, such as that associated with EAP, is referred to as *washback*. Washback usually refers to the impact which tests have on teaching professionals, test takers and educational environments. It is also frequently described as 'the tail wagging the dog' when tests  influence a syllabus or teaching approach, rather than the other way around.

Washback has the propensity to be positive in situations where the influence of testing requirements has a beneficial impact on classroom instruction. Such occurrences may involve increased motivation through test-taker preparedness (Green, 2007, p. 6).

Task 1

- Consider your own EAP context: in what circumstances has the impact of a future EAP assessment had a positive impact on your classroom focus? Perhaps it has given focus to your syllabus or given your students an external target to work towards.
- At what point does the influence of a test start to have a negative impact, in your view? What is the difference between exam technique and the start of negative washback?

Negative influences of washback

Despite the possible positive influences of washback, generally, there seem to be fewer examples referred to (Cheng, Watanabe & Curtis, 2004). Washback seems to be more frequently referenced where there are negative circumstances and when the need for people to take tests has resulted in classroom activity that has detracted from the achievement of more purposeful or practical learning outcomes which reflect the target domain.

Task 2

- How are you and your students influenced by washback from assessments associated with EAP tests? Consider possible washback from external standardized tests and from the EAP assessments which are created within your own department.
- Does washback influence both the content that you teach and the methodology of your teaching practice?
- Is the washback that you experience negative or positive in nature? If the washback is negative, how could you limit the negative impact?
- Washback can sometimes be linked to external pressures or institutional requirements. How is this the case in EAP?
- Is there any washback which affects how you communicate and explain the results of your EAP assessments?

Wall and Alderson (1993) describe an investigation in a Sri Lankan classroom which was initially developed with the expectation that it would demonstrate the positive impact of new tests on classroom practice. Unfortunately, when the research findings were analyzed, it showed that the test washback was less positive than originally envisaged.

Task 3

- Think of a particular EAP test that you have introduced in the past, and consider the impact this may have had on your own teaching context and the studies of your students. Could this test have influenced the students' study in a less than purposeful manner?
- In some learning contexts, teachers and students equate the study of EAP with practising tests and question types which aren't necessarily representative of how EAP will be used in a real university or educational context. Why might this be problematic?

Washback and domain underrepresentation

Washback is perhaps most concerning when tests, such as those used in EAP contexts, are used for admission or selection purposes, as test takers may become motivated to gain the skills that are required to do well in that test, rather than those which are an accurate representation of the target academic domain which they are working towards (Green, 2007).

The problem arises as the skills that are necessary to pass an examination or assessment may not always be a comprehensive reflection of the target language use domain (Bachman & Palmer, 1996).

Task 4

- Consider your experience of students who have joined your EAP programme or university through having taken an external test linked to EAP. What sort of skills have they acquired? Are they similar to those required in the real university context?

- Do you feel that the tests and scores which are accepted by your admissions team have predictive validity with respect to how students will cope on your programmes?

- How could the test tasks embedded within external measures be enhanced, in your view?

- How could the admissions team gain a better understanding of the skills and aptitude of the students that wish to join your programmes? What challenges might be involved?

Washback and the exertion of power

For critical language-testing experts, such as Shohamy (2001), washback is associated with the power exerted by large examination boards and educational companies which purposefully seek to control the behaviours of institutions like universities and their staff.

According to Taylor (2005), some language testers see washback as part of impact, and refer to the repercussions for the educational settings (Hamp-Lyons, 1997), whilst others position washback and impact as quite different phenomena that are distinguished by corresponding 'micro' and 'macro' effects in the societies in which they are located.

In practice, testing professionals link washback to construct validity and the broader consequences of assessment (Messick, 1989).

Task 5

- To what extent do you feel that the construct validity of your EAP teaching and assessment has been influenced or constrained by practices associated with external or institutional assessment models?

- How have you managed any challenges that you have faced in such situations?

Governmental policy and EAP assessment washback

One aspect of EAP testing washback which is triggered by forces beyond those of testing companies and examination boards can be linked to government policy and the identification of the types of test which are permissible for visa purposes. For example, in the UK, it is no longer possible to admit international students to pre-degree programmes or pre-sessional language courses without students having gained a satisfactory score through assessments, taken at a restricted range of test centres, which are centrally listed as being one of a series of Secure English Language Tests.

This single policy change has prevented the use of institutions' in-house EAP testing mechanisms for visa purposes. This outcome demonstrates how the change of policy relating to language testing can impact a range of different stakeholders, including international students and test development, and related research within universities; it also changes the equilibrium in terms of knowledge and power (Foucault, 1977; Foucault & Gordon, 1980).

Although O'Sullivan (2011, pp. 265–270) acknowledges the potential threats to test quality if teachers' Assessment Literacy is limited during the development of local in-house tests, certain benefits are also mentioned regarding the local contexts in which many in-house tests are created. Rea-Dickins, Kiely and Yu, in O'Sullivan (2011), argue that, in most situations, local tests are more likely to allow practitioners to make valid assumptions about test takers.

This modern-day example highlights both the range of political considerations which have come to be associated with language testing and the restriction which this situation places on the EAP profession in terms of providing opportunities for staff to develop skills in assessment through professional practice.

Task 6

- Has the washback from testing-related policy at government level ever had an impact on your own EAP teaching and assessment practices? If so, in what way(s)?

- How have you managed any challenges that you have faced in such situations?

- If your EAP teaching involves preparing students for study overseas, how has your teaching and assessment been impacted by the policies of governments in the countries where your students wish to study?
- Have your students benefitted from changes to government policy, or have these changes resulted in less positive changes in your classroom activity?
- Do you have any recommendations for how the governmental policy could be changed to benefit the stakeholders involved?

Washback from standardized EAP testing systems

Another potential factor relating to negative washback of EAP assessment involves university administrator familiarity with and preference for common standardized test scoring formats and band scores.

An example is provided by an account of practices at a UK university (Banerjee & Wall, 2006), which explains how the reporting of EAP grades using a system based on the band scores used by a large-scale standardized test was abandoned in favour of writing a profile report for each student due to concerns relating to reliability.

Whilst university admissions colleagues in this particular context may have appreciated the face validity of scores which appeared similar to the band scores of popular standardized tests, these were ultimately deemed unsuitable by EAP practitioners, as the in-house tests were different to the external standardized testing system.

The rating scales and marking criteria for the external test's papers were not all uniformly accessible or available in the public domain and the teaching team had not been trained to assess the external EAP test.

Task 7

- Has your EAP assessment process ever been influenced or constrained by administrative requirements relating to student records or admissions systems? If so, how have you managed such situations and how would you advise other colleagues who face similar challenges at different institutions?
- Do you have to report your students' EAP grades using band scores used by external testing systems? If so, how do you know that they are equivalent, given that full criteria are not always available in the public domain?
- Do you create more detailed grade reports to assist students and staff in understanding their performance in tests?

Experiences of washback

Colleagues involved in EAP assessment may experience washback in a range of ways during their careers in teaching and assessment. Figure 1 below provides a series of views related to washback in EAP assessment, which may reflect some of your own experiences.

> Standardized EAP tests are all-pervasive; they're in every country that you go to and people are training to take these tests and to answer set questions, rather than actually learning the language and the broader set of skills. The results of these tests also seem to be very variable.

> Somewhere like China, you just see the sheer volume; you don't get the same idea in Britain at all. These commercially available EAP tests are like a kind of machine which processes thousands of students every month … So, that is an impact of these exams that I personally find very problematic in terms of trying to help someone really develop their skills.

> I have encountered negative washback many times in my career. The things that you're testing the students on are not necessarily the things that are covered on the course that has been taught.

> I aim to create writing tasks in my teaching and assessment which create positive washback. For example, in many situations, discursive essays are not relevant. We need to use assessment models which reflect what students are actually going to have to do in their academic study.

> By the time students get to university, they have already trained for standardized EAP tests so much that they find it difficult to move away from the restricted view that they have experienced. In a sense, I think there's no point fighting the external forces behind these testing organizations, as they are an unavoidable symptom of the marketization of education.

Figure 1: Experiences of washback

Task 8

- How do the views expressed in Figure 1 compare to your own experiences of washback in EAP assessment?
- What suggestions do you have for improving some of the negative situations which are created through washback?
- Do you agree that washback is 'an unavoidable symptom of the marketization of education'?

Building EAP test

Extension activities

> The following extension activities can be exploited by colleagues who have additional time to explore and develop the strategies and principles introduced in this chapter.

» Survey your EAP students to gain a better understanding of how they have been affected by washback through the EAP assessment that they have experienced in their lives, both prior to and during study at your institution. When you have analyzed the results, try to identify ways to build on positive experiences that they have had and how to address any more limiting or negative washback experiences.

» Ask students to work in groups to create a poster comparing and contrasting their training and experiences of EAP teaching and assessment prior to studying at your institution. Once they have identified some differences, help them to see how the gaps in their knowledge or the restricted constructs which they have focused on will be expanded upon and broadened through their current or forthcoming studies.

» At the start of your programmes, modules or courses, discuss with your students the experiences of EAP assessment that they have had to date and show them how the constructs which are embedded within some popular standardized tests can differ from the broader constructs and target learning outcomes which are built into EAP study in your context. This can assist students in understanding the wider scope of the use of EAP in real academic situations.

» Demonstrate the pitfalls of test-driven learning to students by describing an assessment preparation scenario which only covers a restricted view of a particular domain. You could use an example from EAP or outside of EAP to illustrate your point. For instance, you could start by using an example from cookery, whereby someone prepares for a cooking competition by repeatedly practising a single cake recipe. The point can then be illustrated by the person's confusion on the day of the cooking competition when a different recipe is presented which then challenges the breadth of skills which have been acquired.

Stakeholder support – 'Did you know …?'

Once you have applied the strategies and principles in this chapter to your EAP assessment context, the following information can be photocopied or adapted for use with different stakeholder groups, such as test takers, parents and staff, who are involved in or affected by your EAP testing and assessment. Consider how this passage could be modified or applied in your own working context.

PHOTOCOPIABLE

Did you know …

that we prioritize meaningful and applied learning on our EAP courses. Whilst we understand the importance of assessment, we actively seek to avoid situations where learning is negatively influenced by training for EAP tests?

Assessment is an unavoidable element of EAP courses in many institutions today, as students often need to demonstrate their proficiency or level in order to apply.

Nevertheless, the ethos of our EAP programmes has at its heart the key objective to develop students' skills in a manner which will assist them, in a more comprehensive manner, to use language and academic skills to their best advantage in their academic study.

We understand that in high-stakes situations, passing a test can sometimes start to dominate the ambitions of students and teachers in a way which may detract from the breadth of learning required for the application of EAP skills in more complex real-world contexts.

As a result, we try to make sure that our syllabus and the associated assessments are appropriately designed so as to reflect the complexity of the learning targets and usage requirements of our students' future academic studies.

When students join our courses, we try to assist them in seeing how their studies with us will introduce them to a broader set of EAP skills which have a wider range of applications than those which are commonly incorporated into external standardized tests. Such external tests often have to be designed for use by a larger cross-section of test takers based in different locations all over the world.

One benefit of the EAP courses and assessments which we provide is that we can build assessments which represent the challenges that our students will face on future courses at our institutions. We can also use these assessments within our courses in ways which support, rather than steer, learning.

References

Bachman, L. F., & Palmer, A. S. (1996). *Language testing in practice: Designing and developing useful language tests.* Oxford: Oxford University Press.

Banerjee, J., & Wall, D. (2006). Assessing and reporting performances on pre-sessional EAP courses: Developing a final assessment checklist and investigating its validity. *Journal of English for Academic Purposes, 5*(1), 50–69.

Cheng, L., Watanabe, Y. J., & Curtis, A. (2004). *Washback in language testing: Research contexts and methods.* Mahwah, N.J.: Lawrence Erlbaum.

Foucault, M. (1977). *Discipline and punish: The birth of the prison.* London: Penguin.

Foucault, M., & Gordon, C. (1980). *Power/knowledge: Selected interviews and other writings, 1972/1977.* Brighton: Harvester Press.

Green, A. (2007). *IELTS washback in context: Preparation for academic writing in higher education.* Cambridge: Cambridge University Press.

Hamp-Lyons, L. (1997). Washback, impact and validity: Ethical concerns. *Language Testing, 14*(3), 295–303.

Messick, S. (1989). Validity. In R. L. Linn (Ed.), *Educational measurement* (3rd ed., p. 610). New York: American Council on Education.

O'Sullivan, B. (Ed.). (2011). *Language testing: Theories and practices.* Basingstoke: Palgrave Macmillan.

Rea-Dickins, P., Kiely, R., & Yu, G. (2011). Uses and impact of test scores in university admissions processes: The language test as the 'hard' criterion. In B. O'Sullivan (Ed.), *Language testing: Theories and practices* (pp. 262–281). Basingstoke: Palgrave Macmillan.

Shohamy, E. (2001). *The power of tests: A critical perspective on the uses of language tests.* Harlow: Longman.

Taylor, L. (2005). Washback and impact. *ELT Journal, 59*(2), 154–155.

Wall, D., & Alderson, J. C. (1993). Examining washback: The Sri Lankan impact study. *Language Testing, 10*, 41–69.

Chapter 12: Ethics

This chapter will:
- introduce you to a range of ethical considerations associated with EAP assessment.
- invite you to explore the ethicality of your own practice in EAP assessment.

You will have the opportunity to:
- consider how your approach to ethical assessment could be enhanced.
- reflect on the impact which EAP assessment may have on the lives of stakeholders who are affected.
- refer to models for an ethical approach which could be implemented in your own work situation.

Handle with care!

Spolsky (1981) may be considered to be one of the first researchers to refer to the ethicality of test use and to discuss the political purposes for which language testing is sometimes used. In Spolsky's view (1981, p. 20), language tests should be given a health warning similar to those given to dangerous drugs or chemicals. This is particularly significant in the context of EAP, given the important gate-keeping function which it performs, institutionally,

nationally and internationally (Flowerdew & Peacock, 2001, p. 192) and the effect that poor assessment or assessment-related decisions can have on people's lives.

In particular, this includes larger-scale standardized tests which offer a clear example of high-stakes tests with social effects (Spolsky, 2012), given the gate-keeping function which they provide in facilitating or withholding access to university study.

Task 1
- Do you agree that language tests, including EAP assessments, should be given a health warning?
- Have you experienced unethical practice associated with EAP testing?
- If you have experienced unethical practice, how did you react to it and did you feel that your voice was heard?
- In what ways can people's lives be affected if EAP testing goes wrong?

Such is the concern regarding test ethicality, that some practitioners (Lynch, 1997; Lynch & Shaw, 2005) have designed alternative approaches to language testing in an attempt to avoid the inherent unethical practices which they believe accompany the power imbalance present in traditional testing systems.

Research undertaken by Shohamy (1998, pp. 331–332) shows that there is growing interest in the role played by language testing in society. Consequently, topics such as test ethicality and bias are now being discussed in research, publications and conferences.

A critical approach to assessment

Shohamy (1998, p. 332) advocates a critical approach to language testing which acknowledges that the act of testing is not neutral. Similarly, Bachman (1990) supports this view when he refers to the fact that 'tests are not developed and used in a value-free psychometric test tube; they are virtually always intended to serve the needs of an educational system or of society at large' (p. 279).

Task 2

- Given the forces surrounding EAP assessment and the factors at stake, do you feel that it is feasible to avoid ethical compromises in the current situation which the sector operates?

- How do you manage the needs of your institution with the duty to your students and their EAP study?

- Do you have scope, like Lynch and Shaw (2005), to consider implementing quite different approaches to assessment with the aim of maintaining a high level of ethicality in your EAP assessment practices?

As advised by McNamara and Roever (2006, p. 8), testers need to engage in debate on the consequential application of their tests and need to reflect on test usage after the point of operationalization, in addition to a customary focus on the test development stages. An example relevant to EAP is provided by Shohamy (2001, p. 102), who refers to the impact of an English test in the Middle East used for university entrance, and the anxiety which was caused given the high stakes associated with success.

Errors linked to the uses to which tests are put can be linked directly to damaging sociological implications and harmful repercussions. The work of Shohamy (1998, 2001) and McNamara and Roever (2006) are particularly relevant in this respect, as they warn of the power of tests and the potential harm which can be incurred. In addition, these risks also resonate with Foucault's postmodern concerns (Foucault, 1977; Foucault & Gordon, 1980) connected to the interplay between information-seeking and power relations.

Task 3

- What do you do to try to minimize student anxiety associated with EAP assessment in your own working context?
- Is the ethicality of your assessment actively supported by your institution and department?
- To what extent are you able to challenge existing procedures, models and systems associated with your assessment of EAP?

Equity and democracy in EAP assessment

With more specific reference to the context of EAP assessment and the need for both EAP practitioners and other stakeholders, including students, to be aware of the societal implications of EAP assessment, Benesch (2001, p. 60) encourages the challenging of conventions associated with EAP through a concern regarding power relations and social justice. Benesch believes that current conditions under which EAP is taught and assessed should be interrogated and probed in the interest of equity and democratic participation, both in and outside educational institutions. The ultimate aim of Benesch's work is to assist students in performing well in their academic courses (ibid., p. xvi).

Recently, a manifestation of the potential anxiousness-raising impact of EAP assessment can be illustrated through the regular fluctuation in the range of standardized EAP tests which are acceptable for UKVI visa purposes and study in the UK. Many EAP professionals will be aware of stakeholder feedback to institutions relating to the consequences of such changes in approved tests.

Task 4

- Do you feel that government policy changes have resulted in ethical issues in the context of your recruitment of EAP students?
- Are you aware of certain power relations within the context of your EAP teaching and assessment? If so, what are they and how might they concern you?
- Are you able to approach your EAP practice in the critical and democratic manner which Benesch and Shohamy advocate?

A shift in approach

Building on the social concerns associated with testing practices, Gipps (1994) recognized the need for a 'paradigm shift' (Kuhn, 1970) in order for stakeholders of examinations to consider assessment in new ways which are suitable for our modern-day purposes and understandings. With this aim in mind, the following measures are suggested:

- movement away from the norm-referenced limiting forces of psychometric models which emphasize ranking
- production of descriptions of performance which allow for idiosyncratic approaches to learning
- design of new and richer methods of presenting results using qualitative descriptors, rather than merely figures
- generation of new ways of ensuring reliability and validity due to the changing nature of assessments and their contexts
- consideration of ethical issues in the development and use of tests

Task 5

- To what extent are you able to implement the practices in your EAP context, as recommended above by Gipps?
- If some of the approaches recommended by Gipps are difficult to manage, why is this? How could this situation be changed?
- Could you suggest any amendments or elements to add to the list provided by Gipps in order to improve it or make it more relevant to your own context?

Ethical codes

Davies (1997) claims that language testers are, in general, genuinely interested in ensuring that the tests they work on follow ethical good practice. Furthermore, Bachman (2000) suggests that the solution to ethical misuse of language tests lies in codes of ethical good practice and this is perhaps a key message for Assessment Literacy. Such ethical guidance frameworks do already exist in the form of EALTA's Guidelines for Good Practice (Erickson & Figueras, 2010) and ILTA's Code of Ethics (ILTA, 2000).

In addition, Kunnan (2003) suggests a number of laudable principles for test fairness, such as: 'Principle 2: *The Principle of Beneficence*: A test ought to bring about good in society. Sub principle 1: A test ought to promote good in society by providing test-score information and social impacts that are beneficial to society.'

Task 6

- Which benchmarks do you and your team use to maintain standards of ethicality in your workplace?
- How familiar are you and your team with existing codes of ethics which can be applied to EAP? This might include the resources provided by EALTA and ILTA.
- If you haven't already consulted the resources mentioned, have a look at the code of ethics on the ILTA website and consider if the practices of your department align appropriately.
- Are you confident that your EAP testing conforms to the 'principle of beneficence'? If not, what could you change to make your assessment more compliant?

Responsibility in EAP assessment

The social and economic implications of testing are extended beyond the impact on local communities by Taylor (2009), who stresses the international importance of testing and assessment. Whilst countries with developed educational systems and established public examinations are, in many cases, now investigating further innovations in teaching and learning for the purposes of extending economic and social enhancement, other developing countries are at different stages and seek to follow in the footsteps of developed nations in order to harness education and assessment methods and to benefit from the long-term gain of their societies. As this is the case, the need for societies with developed assessment mechanisms to ensure that practices are sufficiently sophisticated and trustworthy is an even higher priority.

Task 7

- Which aspects of your department's own EAP assessment could be upheld as models of good and ethical practice?
- Which aspects of your assessment do you feel require further attention in order to be considered as ethical practice models?
- What training or skill development would you like to suggest in order to enhance the EAP assessment within your context or department? In which ways to you think this might make a positive difference?

Nonetheless, despite warnings surrounding the risks associated with poor Assessment Literacy and the existence of models of good practice, there still appears to be a sense in the mind of critical language testers (McNamara & Roever, 2006; Shohamy, 2001) that the consciousness of the power of tests needs to be reawakened amongst language testers. Given that some of the most powerful contemporary standardized tests are associated with EAP, this area of concern can be seen as having particular significance.

Task 8

- To what extent are you and your department active in acknowledging the power of EAP assessment, and minimizing negative outcomes?
- Is there more that you could do to support the rights of stakeholders who are affected by EAP assessment in your working context?
- Could you persuade your institution to adapt current practices so that the stakeholders of your EAP assessment are able to benefit?

Evaluating your own practice

Given the importance placed upon ethicality in this chapter, it is clear that a process of evaluation and reflection linked to ethical procedures in EAP assessment could be a step in the right direction. Table 1 could be used as a starting position to gauge you or your team's familiarity with certain ethical considerations linked to EAP assessment.

Table 1: Checklist of ethical considerations

Checklist of ethical considerations	Yes/No/Comments
I am familiar with existing codes of practice for language testing and how they relate to the EAP context.	
There is an active process in my department which promotes the maintenance of ethical standards.	
I am concerned about the social implications of EAP language testing.	
EAP teachers involved in assessment are responsible for evaluating the ethical consequences of the projects that they are involved with.	
I feel able to refuse to participate in procedures which would violate ethical principles of EAP assessment.	
I feel that my employers are sufficiently aware of ethical dilemmas associated with EAP assessment.	
I have recently felt obliged to contribute to EAP testing procedures which I question the ethicality of.	

Task 9

- Complete Table 1 and consider the responses that you have provided. Do you feel that any of your responses might suggest that there are areas within your working context where further consideration could be given to ethics?
- Which areas could be improved on? In which respects does your department perform well?
- Could you devise an internal version of the checklist which is tailored to your own situation and which can be used as an ethical benchmarking tool?

Ethical dilemmas

During the course of our careers as EAP teachers and assessors, we may encounter situations which have ethical implications. These situations can sometimes present dilemmas which are not necessarily straightforward to respond to. Table 2 provides a list of ethical dilemmas which may affect a range of stakeholders in the context of EAP assessment. Each of the dilemmas listed invites a response.

Table 2: Ethical dilemmas

Ethical dilemmas	
1	Chinese students struggle with EAP speaking tests and should be required to gain higher grades in EAP speaking tests from next year.
2	The university has asked to use the Pre-sessional EAP test with a group of international nurses seeking to find employment at a local hospital. The Academic Language Centre should allow this.
3	A security risk has required the evacuation of the building for 15 minutes during Group A's EAP test. As a result, the tests should be marked as they were at the point of evacuation.
4	Two tutors from the EAP team would like to give extra classes to certain students who they feel need to improve their examination technique. This action should be avoided.
5	A university department wants to recruit fewer international students, so the Academic Language Centre should permit the change of the passing grade for current students in its EAP test from 60% to 70%.

6	Government policy has changed, so it is acceptable to tell a current class of EAP students that they either need to improve their admissions scores by 10%, or return home before the end of their EAP course.
7	Unexpectedly, nearly all students fail the final EAP test, so the EAP team should consider adjusting the marks using a bell curve.
8	An EAP tutor is preparing students for an EAP test. It is therefore good practice for the tutor to highlight key skills for revision in the class course textbook.
9	University rules require students to show their library card at the door of the EAP exam room. Wen Hu has lost his library card, so he should not be allowed to enter the room.
10	Students should be encouraged to question the grades they get in EAP tests.

Task 10

- After reading the ethical dilemmas, which of the dilemmas do you feel relate most closely to your own experiences?
- Which of the dilemmas did you find easy to respond to and which were more challenging?
- Were there any listed dilemmas that you didn't know how to respond to?
- Have any of the dilemmas listed caused you to think differently about a similar situation that you have experienced?
- Have you experienced any alternative dilemmas that could be added to the list?
- Discuss the list of dilemmas with your colleagues and reflect on any differences of opinion which may emerge.

Extension activities

The following extension activities can be exploited by colleagues who have additional time to explore and develop the strategies and principles introduced in this chapter.

» After working through this chapter, consider any areas of your working practice in EAP assessment which could be reviewed in terms of ethicality. Consider the position of the different stakeholders who are affected by your EAP assessment and identify ways in which they can be treated more fairly.

» Make a point of referring more frequently to codes of practice or good practice guides such as those referenced in this chapter. Build reference to these resources into the systematic review of your assessments so that you can keep track of any emerging issues.

» Create a platform to assist colleagues or students in identifying and drawing attention to any matters associated with ethics of EAP assessment; this may be an extension of an existing forum or feedback mechanism which you have, such as a staff/student liaison committee or end-of-course feedback tools.

» Work with colleagues to formulate an ethical policy which can be shared with other colleagues within your institution or beyond so that your EAP assessments are used appropriately and your test results are not misconstrued or inaccurately interpreted.

» Consider the ethics associated with your admissions process and how fair it is to accept or reject students at certain grade boundaries. Consider the fullness of the information that you use and the extent to which your decisions are well-founded or fair.

» How ethical and fair is your overall approach to EAP assessment? Can you honestly say that sufficient attention is devoted to the test design, piloting and marking processes? Which aspects need to be improved and which tools, systems or resources might you need?

Stakeholder support – 'Did you know ...?'

Once you have applied the strategies and principles in this chapter to your EAP assessment context, the following information can be photocopied or adapted for use with different stakeholder groups, such as test takers, parents and staff, who are involved in or affected by your EAP testing and assessment. Consider how this passage could be modified or applied in your own working context.

Did you know ...	that we strive to adopt an ethical and fair approach to our EAP assessment, given our understanding of the high-stakes nature of EAP assessment?

Success or failure in the study of EAP can play an important role in students' future careers, given the progression opportunities to other academic programmes and future careers, which may be either granted or removed.

For this reason, we work hard to ensure that the practices associated with our assessment of EAP are ethical and fair, so that our test takers and other stakeholders who work with our students are not disadvantaged in any way.

We take a critical approach to the development, trialling and marking of our assessments, which encourages colleagues to identify problematic situations or faulty questions which may not be appropriately structured or which may disadvantage students or misrepresent true levels of ability.

We are acutely aware that educational measurement can have a negative influence on people's lives if it is not practised in a principled way and we wish to take every step to avoid this situation.

Our department is aware of ethical codes of practice and we practise an approach to equality and diversity which necessarily extends to include our assessment procedures.

References

Bachman, L. F. (1990). *Fundamental considerations in language testing*. Oxford: Oxford University Press.

Bachman, L. F. (2000). Modern language testing at the turn of the century: Assuring that what we count counts. *Language Testing, 17*(1), 1–42.

Benesch, S. (2001). *Critical English for academic purposes: Theory, politics, and practice*. Mahwah, N.J./London: Lawrence Erlbaum Associates.

Davies, A. (1997). Demands of being professional in language testing. *Language Testing, 14*(3), 328–339.

Erickson, G., & Figueras, N. (2010). *EALTA guidelines for good practice in language testing and assessment: Large scale dissemination days*. EALTA.

Flowerdew, J., & Peacock, M. (2001). *Research perspectives on English for academic purposes*. Cambridge: Cambridge University Press.

Foucault, M. (1977). *Discipline and punish: The birth of prison*. London: Penguin.

Foucault, M., & Gordon, C. (1980). *Power/knowledge: Selected interviews and other writings, 1972/1977*. Brighton: Harvester Press.

Gipps, C. (1994). *Beyond testing: Towards a theory of educational assessment*. London: Falmer.

ILTA. (2000). *ILTA code of ethics*. Retrieved from http://www.iltaonline.com

Kuhn, T. S. (1970). *The structure of scientific revolutions* (2nd ed.). Chicago/London: University of Chicago Press.

Kunnan, A. J. (2003). *Test fairness*. Paper presented at the European Year of Language Conference, Barcelona.

Lynch, B. K. (1997). In search of the ethical test. *Language Testing, 14*(3), 315–327.

Lynch, B. K., & Shaw, P. (2005). Portfolios, power and ethics. *TESOL Quarterly, 39*(2), 263–297.

McNamara, T., & Roever, C. (2006). *Language testing: The social dimension*. Oxford: Blackwell.

Shohamy, E. (1998). Critical language testing and beyond. *Studies in Educational Evaluation, 24*(4), 331–345.

Shohamy, E. (2001). *The power of tests: A critical perspective on the uses of language tests*. Harlow: Longman.

Spolsky, B. (1981). Some ethical questions about language testing. In C. Klein-Braley & D. K. Stevenson (Eds.), *Practice and problems in language testing I* (pp. 5–21). Frankfurt: Peter Lang.

Spolsky, B. (2012). Language testing and language management. In F. Davidson & G. Fulcher (Eds.), *The Routledge handbook of language testing* (p. 497). Oxford: Routledge.

Taylor, L. (2009). Developing Assessment Literacy. *Annual Review of Applied Linguistics, 29*, 21–36.

Chapter 13: Building EAP test Assessment Literacy amongst stakeholders

This chapter will:
- demonstrate the importance of assisting stakeholders to understand what the results of EAP tests show.
- highlight the importance of EAP Assessment Literacy amongst different stakeholder groups.

You will have the opportunity to:
- consider the needs of staff and students in terms of EAP Assessment Literacy.
- reflect on implications of government policy on EAP Assessment Literacy.
- identify opportunities for supporting the stakeholders within your own institution more effectively.

The importance of helping others to understand the results of EAP tests

Whilst many higher education professionals are aware of some of the features of commercial standardized EAP tests and what their results imply, it is necessary to recognize that in-house testing systems, developed and used within universities, also play a key institutional gate-keeping role. On the completion of EAP courses or programmes which include an EAP element, students may either meet or fail to meet linguistic thresholds and can sometimes be turned away from their intended programmes of study.

As a result, it is important to ensure that other users of any form of EAP test-results, in addition to EAP teachers and test creators, have as much information as possible relating to the assessment and what it claims to demonstrate about test takers' skills. This, therefore, suggests a critical need for EAP practitioners and other users of EAP test scores who are 'in the know' to help build competence across institutions in identifying features of reliable or unreliable measures of EAP. Training interventions and documents such as test reports and specifications can potentially assist admissions teams in properly understanding the results of EAP tests. This need for a dynamic response resonates with Popham's (2001, 2006) call for proactivity in the training of educators and other stakeholders. Such sentiments also explain why organizations such as BALEAP are keen to promote high standards of assessment in EAP.

Task 1

- How informed do you feel admissions tutors and administrators are at your institution regarding what commercial standardized tests claim to demonstrate?
- How much interest is shown in reports relating to students' ability which might accompany numerical or band-based EAP test scores?
- Have you experienced unethical practice associated with EAP testing?
- How active is your department in sharing knowledge about EAP tests and what their results show across your institution?

Implications of government policy for EAP Assessment Literacy

As an example from the UK, one of the key implications for universities seeking to use their own in-house testing systems for admissions purposes, since 2011, relates to a specific government policy concerning the types of test which are permissible for study visa issuance linked to particular levels of academic study. Given the complex and shifting nature of changes to government-related policy, since 2010, some UK universities have been less active in the development and use of their own EAP tests for university admissions purposes.

This outcome highlights how the changes to government policy relating to language testing can impact a range of different stakeholders, including international students and scholarly activity associated with EAP test development at UK universities. Rea-Dickins, Kiely and Yu in O'Sullivan (2011) argue that, in most situations, local tests are more likely to allow practitioners to make valid assumptions about test takers. It is also suggested that local test developers have opportunities to focus on specific domains and contexts which fit with local needs. However, if universities are discouraged from engagement in activity connected to the development of EAP tests and assessments, there is arguably a restriction on the EAP profession in terms of mechanisms for developing Assessment Literacy through professional practice. O'Sullivan (2011, pp. 265–270) also acknowledges potential threats to in-house-designed EAP test quality and claims relating to levels of student proficiency, if EAP teachers' Assessment Literacy is limited during the development of local EAP tests.

Task 2

- Has your institution been significantly affected by any governmental policy changes in your country or region? If so, how? Has the experience been positive or negative? Has there been an impact on other stakeholders? Do you think the changes should be maintained or reversed?

- Are you aware of any EAP tests developed by other universities which may have had to change their approach in how their tests are used?

- What do you think about external standardized tests and in-house EAP tests and how they compare in terms of reliability and validity?

- Do you agree or disagree that your own Assessment Literacy development may have been compromised due to stricter government regulation?

Assessment Literacy of decision-makers in higher education

Evidence suggests that, along with the growth of internationalization of higher education and the widespread use of EAP tests and examinations as part of the admissions process, there is a need for the sharing of information between assessors of EAP and other colleagues who process applications and make offers for university entry. In a presentation at a conference of the Association of Language Testers in Europe (ALTE) (Baker, 2014), a Language Assessment Literacy project was referenced which is currently underway in Canada. This project, undertaken by a researcher working at McGill University, aims to bridge the gap between language assessment specialists, researchers and developers, and the people who make use of language test scores. The project aims to cultivate greater collaboration with admissions decision-makers at higher education institutions. The phases of the project involve developing, administering and analyzing a survey to admissions officers, creating a series of training workshops and analyzing feedback from participants. Baker (2014) and Baker, Tsushima and Wang (2014) also refer to a range of other research material which highlights the need for further training for individuals making high-stakes decisions based on language assessments. These include:

- O'Loughlin (2011, 2013) (IELTS): Assessment Literacy of university stakeholders and the use of EAP grades in admissions decision-making

- Ginther and Elder (2013) (TOEFL, IELTS and PTE): Reports from admissions officers regarding limited knowledge for the use and interpretation of these tests

- Rea-Dickins, Kiely and Yu (2007) (IELTS): University admissions staff who are not always sufficiently knowledgeable about the meaning of standardized test scores

- Hyatt and Brooks (2009): Describe a lack of knowledge amongst admissions stakeholders

Task 3

- How EAP assessment literate are admissions decision-makers at your institution?
- Is your department consulted regarding external measures of EAP?
- Could you get involved with training related to EAP Assessment Literacy for stakeholders across your institution?
- Would you be able to work with admissions tutors or administrators in a collaborative manner, such as the Canadian university mentioned in this chapter (Baker, 2014 and Baker et al., 2014)?

Admissions administrator familiarity with standardized EAP test formats

Another factor relating to reliability of EAP assessment which is relevant for EAP Assessment Literacy involves the negative washback of university administrator familiarity with standardized test scoring formats. An example is provided by Banerjee and Wall (2006), regarding practices at one particular university where the reporting of in-house EAP test grades using a band system based on a popular standardized test was abandoned, due to concerns about reliability, in favour of writing a profile report for each student. Whilst other university admissions colleagues within the university may have appreciated the face validity of scores which appeared familiar to a system that they already knew, these were ultimately deemed unsuitable by EAP practitioners for the reasons listed below.

- The official rating scales for the external standardized test for speaking and writing were not available.

- Estimating reading and listening abilities was problematic, since this depended on inferences about students' 'inner processes', rather than analyses of products such as essays or oral presentations.

- None of the EAP teaching team had been trained as examiners for the standardized test.

Task 4

- How reliant are your colleagues on comparisons of internal test results with external measures of EAP proficiency?
- Are you required to convert your results into a grade or band which looks like a system used by an external test provider? If so, how are you able to do this scientifically?

Students and their EAP Assessment Literacy

Members of the Assessment Knowledge Standards exchange (ASKe) (2013), a Centre for Excellence in Teaching and Learning (CETL) based at Oxford Brookes University, have been investigating assessment practices in higher education over the last two decades, with a view to promoting the importance of Assessment Literacy, with a particular emphasis on student involvement. This research is undertaken by experts with a range of experience of working with international students, so the relevance to the EAP context is strong.

Whilst the impact on stakeholders, particularly students and test takers, is always central to the promotion of Assessment Literacy, as acknowledged by Stiggins (1991; 1995) and Popham (2001), Price, Rust, O'Donovan and Handley (2012) from ASKe offer a particularly prominent focus on the importance of fostering the Assessment Literacy of students and their understanding of the mechanisms of assessment. This view of the critical agenda for Assessment Literacy emphasizes the broader definition of assessment and refers not only to measurement of achievement, but also to the accessibility and interpretability of feedback, as well as the giving of support and development of student learning. This approach towards formative assessment shares attributes with Assessment for Learning (Biggs & Tang, 2011, p. 64; Knight, 1995), as mentioned earlier.

The stance adopted by Price et al. (2012) acknowledges the fact that, the more students understand what is expected of them in the assessment process, the more likely they will be to meet the demands of the assessment mechanisms they experience. It is also recognized that assessment is central to the student experience and that student satisfaction ratings for assessment and feedback in higher education remain less than optimal. Price et al. (ibid., p. 10) describe Assessment Literacy in terms of knowledge, skills and competencies. In this view, Assessment Literacy encompasses an appreciation of the purposes and processes of assessment, which allows deep engagement with assessment standards and the making of choices about which skill or area of knowledge to apply. This facilitates an understanding of situations when aspects of assessment are appropriate or inappropriate. This definition of Assessment Literacy extends to include:

- an appreciation of assessment's relationship to learning;
- a conceptual understanding of assessment (i.e., understanding of the basic principles of valid assessment and feedback practice, including terminology used);
- an understanding of the nature, meaning and level of assessment criteria and standards;
- skills in self- and peer-assessment;
- a familiarity with technical approaches to assessment (e.g., pertinent assessment and feedback skills, techniques and methods, including their purpose and efficacy); and
- the possession of the intellectual ability to select and apply appropriate approaches and techniques to assessed tasks (which skill to use when, and for what).

Task 5

- How much effort do you put into assisting students to understand their EAP grades and test results?
- Do your students understand what they are being assessed on, and how and why they are being assessed? How do you achieve this? Could you do this better?
- How do you help students to act on their weaknesses and hone their strengths?
- How do you react if a student challenges your approach to EAP assessment or the way in which they have been marked or graded? Is this encouraged?

A lot of time, admissions tutors just look at the final EAP score and that final score needs to tell them if the student is good enough or not good enough.

For us as EAP teachers, much more emphasis is placed on feedback, rather than the final grade.

Well, I don't always have time to feed back on marks and to highlight what students have achieved.

Despite the CEFR, I feel like I have to try to equate my students' level to an IELTS score, so that the university that the student goes to will have an understanding of their level.

I used to spend a lot of time writing detailed feedback, but students just seem to want the final grade, so now I must admit I don't put as much effort into it as I used to.

What we find is that the raw EAP test results just offer one kind of 'quick and dirty' answer. They're not enough on their own.

We end up saying it's equivalent to, you know, IELTS 7.5 or whatever, you know, and I want to stop doing that because, you know, it isn't.

We give feedback on students' EAP assessments and tests so they will understand them as best we can explain, in terms of formative feedback.

Figure 1: Comments relating to EAP test stakeholders and Assessment Literacy

Task 6

- Read the comments in Figure 1 and consider the extent to which they relate to situations which you have experienced in your EAP practice.
- Write a series of comments yourself, or collect a series of anonymous comments from your department, in order to gauge the situation in your own department and institution.
- What could you do better as an individual and as a department to provide better information and support to your stakeholders, relating to EAP Assessment Literacy?

Extension activities

The following extension activities can be exploited by colleagues who have additional time to explore and develop the strategies and principles introduced in this chapter.

» On completing this chapter, consider any additional ways in which you could help your colleagues and stakeholders of EAP assessments to better understand the range of skills which your test scores represent, so that students' abilities can be understood, as well as possible.

» Work together with counterparts in different departments, both academic and administrative, to develop an approach to understanding EAP assessments which benefits your institution as a whole. You could arrange a reciprocal shadowing exercise with a colleague working in admissions so that you can understand better their approach to EAP-related admissions decisions.

» Consider offering a centrally advertised training session for admissions tutors and administrators, based on understanding external EAP assessment mechanisms.

» Encourage your institution to make more use of the CEFR and to move away from understanding grades in terms of the reporting systems of commercial tests. Although the CEFR is not a perfect model, there is more openly available benchmarking information than can be found for commercial tests, for which full details are not often released in the public domain. If possible, try to lobby for the time and resources to undertake a benchmarking activity related to your EAP assessment.

» Work with colleagues in your department or in similar departments across different institutions in order to share good practice in EAP assessment development. Looking at each other's tests could act as useful a form of continuing professional development (CPD).

» Put yourself forward as an external examiner so that you can gain an insight into the EAP assessment practices at another institution.

Stakeholder support – 'Did you know ...?'

Once you have applied the strategies and principles in this chapter to your EAP assessment context, the following information can be photocopied or adapted for use with different stakeholder groups, such as test takers, parents and staff, who are involved in or affected by your EAP testing and assessment. Consider how this passage could be modified or applied in your own working context.

Did you know ...	that we try to build Assessment Literacy amongst both student and staff stakeholders, so that the abilities of students can be more fully understood and taken into account?

As part of our approach to EAP assessment, we understand that it is important to promote Assessment Literacy amongst both student and staff stakeholder groups.

In this way, if people understand why they are being assessed and what the results of assessments show in terms of EAP skills and abilities, then it is possible to use this information in a more principled manner and to make the right kind of decisions and choices accordingly.

With regard to EAP students and test takers, if members of this group understand the assessments that they are taking and the grades which are returned, then they can also identify which EAP constructs are being measured at different points. As a result, students and test takers can then also draw on the appropriate aspects of their skill sets in order to answer questions or to demonstrate their EAP capabilities. By understanding as much about EAP tests as possible, this can also assist test takers in understanding their strengths and weaknesses better, so that these can be harnessed as part of the process of ongoing learning.

As far as staff stakeholders are concerned, encouraging Assessment Literacy involves taking test results beyond marks or percentages in order to develop a more rounded and informative impression of students' abilities, so that they can be evaluated more effectively in the process of high-stakes decision-making.

We understand that both students and staff groups at institutions which teach and use EAP test results are often very busy. Similarly, we recognize the importance of lifting test grades off the page so that people are not unfairly represented by one-dimensional or unreliable figures.

References

ASKe. (2013). *Assessment standards knowledge exchange.* Retrieved from http://www.brookes.ac.uk/aske/

Baker, B. A. (April, 2014). *Determining the language assessment literacy of admissions decision makers in higher education.* Paper presented at ALTE, Paris.

Baker, B. A., Tsushima, R., & Wang, S. (2014). Investigating language assessment literacy: Collaboration between assessment specialists and Canadian university admissions officers. *Language Learning in Higher Education, 4*(1), 137–157.

Banerjee, J., & Wall, D. (2006). Assessing and reporting performances on pre-sessional EAP courses: Developing a final assessment checklist and investigating its validity. *Journal of English for Academic Purposes, 5*(1), 50–69.

Biggs, J. B., & Tang, C. S. (2011). *Teaching for quality learning at university: What the student does* (4ᵗʰ ed.). Maidenhead: McGraw-Hill/Society for Research into Higher Education/Open University Press.

Ginther, A., & Elder, C. (2013). *The use and interpretation of English proficiency test scores in the graduate admissions process.* Paper presented at EALTA, Istanbul. Retrieved from http://www.ealta.eu.org/conference/2013/presentations/Ginther%20and%20Elder%20presentat_on%20EALTA%202013.pdf

Hyatt, D., & Brooks, G. (2009). Investigating stakeholders' perceptions of IELTS as an entry requirement for higher education in the UK. *IELTS Research Reports, 10,* 17–68.

Knight, P. (1995). *Assessment for learning in higher education.* London: Kogan Page.

O'Loughlin, K. (2011). The interpretation and use of proficiency test scores in university selection: How valid and ethical are they? *Language Assessment Quarterly, 8*(2), 146–160.

O'Loughlin, K. (2013). Developing the assessment literacy of university proficiency test users. *Language Testing, 30*(3), 363–380.

O'Sullivan, B. (Ed.) (2011). *Language testing: Theories and practices.* Basingstoke: Palgrave Macmillan.

Popham, W. J. (2001). *The truth about testing: An educator's call to action.* Alexandria, VA: ASCD.

Popham, W. J. (2006). Needed: A dose of assessment literacy. *Educational Leadership, 63*(6), 84–85. Retrieved from http://www.ascd.org/publications/educationalleadership/mar06/vol63/num06/Needed@-A-Dose-of-Assessment-Literacy.aspx

Price, M., Rust, C., O'Donovan, B., & Handley, K. (2012). *Assessment literacy: The foundation for improving student learning.* Oxford: Oxford Brookes University.

Rea-Dickins, P., Kiely, R., & Yu, G. (2007). Student identity, learning and progression (SILP): The affective and academic impact of IELTS on "successful candidates". *IELTS Research Reports, 7,* 59–136.

Rea-Dickins, P., Kiely, R., & Yu, G. (2011). Uses and impact of test scores in university admissions processes: The language test as the 'hard' criterion. In B. O'Sullivan (Ed.), *Language testing: Theories and practices* (pp. 262–281). London: Palgrave Macmillan.

Stiggins, R. J. (1991). Assessment Literacy. *The Phi Delta Kappan, 72*(7), 534.

Stiggins, R. J. (1995). Assessment Literacy for the 21st Century. *The Phi Delta Kappan,* 77(3), 238.

Chapter 14: Learning from large-scale standardized EAP tests

This chapter will:

- identify examples of how experience of external standardized tests can inform the assessment practice of EAP practitioners.
- highlight a number of research-related developments which are mirrored in changes made over time to well-known tests that are linked to EAP.

You will have the opportunity to:

- consider how knowledge and experience of standardized EAP testing systems can contribute to EAP professional development.
- reflect on the implications of changes and innovations which have emerged in standardized EAP testing systems and what impact these have for test takers and test validity.

The role of standardized EAP testing agencies

Standardized and commercial testing agencies play an undeniably important role in the modern global education village, measuring the language skills of international students seeking to study through the medium of English in higher education (McNamara, 2000, p. 24). Such high-stakes and commercially operated tests, which claim to be standardized and often appear to have strong face validity, are ever  growing in impact (ibid: Blue, Milton & Saville, 2000, p. 8). It is, therefore, logical that familiarity with large-scale assessment practices associated with standardized EAP tests will form part of the EAP teachers' Assessment Literacy toolkit.

Task 1

- In what ways do you think standardized tests linked to EAP play an important role in higher education?
- To what extent has your EAP test development practice been informed by your knowledge of external standardized tests?
- Which good practices have you learnt or adopted?

- Which aspects or features of external EAP tests would you seek to avoid in your own EAP test practice?
- Have you ever worked as an examiner for a commercial testing board? Was this a useful experience for your own training as an EAP assessor?

A standardized test should ideally demonstrate the following characteristics as listed below in Table 1. However, it should be noted that not all tests which are commonly referred to as 'standardized' meet these criteria to the same extent.

Table 1: Characteristics of standardized tests (extended from the original definition in Davies, Brown, Elder, Hill, Lumley & McNamara, 1999, p. 187)

Criterion	Description
Rigorous development	• Research and piloting/trialling to determine the measurement properties of the test • Principled sampling from the population and domain of interest • Definition of the measurement scale • Establishing adequate reliability and validity • Careful identification of norms for the population, based on score distribution • Statistical equating of all forms of the test so that any scores reported always represent the same level of ability
Standard procedures for administration and scoring	• Development of procedures for test administration and test conditions which can be shared across different test centres • Training for markers, including moderation and use of criteria • Transformation of raw scores into other forms, such as percentages, bands for ease of interpretation or use
Standard test content	• Use of test specifications which describe areas such as test content, item types, test structure/design and language constructs so that test versions can be designed to meet the same assessment objectives

Despite varying stances towards the suitability of any particular externally provided standardized testing system, and the powerful influences that such assessments can have on individuals and institutions (Shohamy, 2001), there is a strong case to argue that the well-known tests which claim to assess EAP do still serve to heighten practitioner awareness and experience of language testing in the context of academic language use. An important impact can be considered to be the facility for EAP teachers to critique and gain inspiration from large-scale commercially provided assessments. This process can arguably inform the development of local or in-house EAP testing systems.

Task 2

- To what extent do your own EAP assessment practices mirror those qualities of standardized assessment, as listed in Table 1?
- Which qualities or features would you like to improve in your own EAP assessments?
- In your own experience of external standardized EAP assessments, which characteristics of standardized tests are most evident and most positive? Which areas are sometimes more questionable or require further development, according to your own experience?

A review of a number of key lessons that can be learnt from the development of three important and internationally renowned EAP-related standardized tests, TOEFL, IELTS and PTE Academic, is included in the sections below.

Lessons in EAP assessment from TOEFL

Originally known more fully as Test of English as a Foreign Language, TOEFL was introduced in the USA in the early 1960s as a means of screening non-native speakers of English for university admissions purposes. The test was devised with the support of the National Council on the Testing of English as a Foreign Language. The Educational Testing Service (ETS) joined forces with the College Board in 1965 in order to share responsibility for TOEFL (ETS, 2011). Table 2 summarizes some of the key evolutionary developments which the TOEFL test has undergone since the 1960s.

Table 2: The evolution of the TOEFL test constructs and contents over three stages of development (ETS, 2011)

Stages	Construct	Content
The First TOEFL Test 1964–1979	Discrete components of language skills and knowledge	Multiple-choice items assessing vocabulary, reading comprehension, listening comprehension, knowledge of correct English structure and grammar.
A Suite of TOEFL Tests 1979–2005	Original constructs (listening, reading, structure and grammar) retained, but two additional ones added: writing ability and speaking ability	In addition to multiple-choice items assessing the original constructs, separate constructed-response tests of writing (the TWE test) and speaking (the TSE test) were developed.

The TOEFL iBT Test 2005–present	Communicative competence – the ability to put language knowledge to use in relevant contexts	Academic tasks were developed that require the integration of receptive and productive skills such as listening, reading and writing or speaking, as well as multiple-choice items for listening and reading.

Taylor and Angelis' (2008) account of the amendments and extensions made to TOEFL over the last four decades aligns with the information provided in Table 2. The developments described in this biography provide a thorough narrative of how research in the fields of language testing and psychological measurement has affected the TOEFL test.

Indeed, by tracking the changes which have been implemented to the content and construct of TOEFL, the contemporary EAP practitioner involved in assessment can track many of the developments attributed to the rise of importance of construct validity, which is perhaps the most influential overarching concept in modern-day good practice for language testing. In this way, the history of TOEFL can be considered as a key resource in the development of EAP Assessment Literacy.

Whilst the enhancements introduced by ETS since TOEFL's original introduction include a number of notable enhancements, Table 2 does not fully describe the forces behind many of these changes. Another factor which is worthwhile considering is the growth of TOEFL test-related high-stakes implications and potential washback in the EAP classroom (Alderson & Hamp-Lyons,1996; Shohamy, 2001, p. 123) such washback has also arguably led to incidences of local malpractice in certain test centres.

Spolsky (1995, pp. 217–333) describes developments in TOEFL from a different perspective and refers to the gradual erosion of TOEFL's independence, including its takeover by the powerful organizations which control it today (McNamara, 1996). As Shohamy (2001, p. 123) explains, the symbolic power of TOEFL is compounded as it symbolizes both a test and the power of the English language. Similar post-modern concerns are extended by Foucault (1977), who states that '... the examination is at the centre of the procedures that constitute the individual as effect and object of power ... It is the examination which, by combining hierarchical surveillance and normalizing judgement, assures the great disciplinary functions of distribution and classification ...' (p. 192). Notably, both these views are somewhat in contrast with the ethos of an exam which provides meritocratic access to university (Fulcher, 2009).

One of the key ways in which the TOEFL test structure has altered since its original introduction was the addition, in the 1980s – due to pressure from language teachers – of the Test of Written English (TWE). Up to this point, ETS claimed that the delivery and reliability of such a written test would be impractical (Hughes, 2003,

p. 6). However, this has clearly not proved to be the case and it is possible that the delay in the introduction of this test component may have been related to matters other than academic impracticality. Interestingly, on a similar note, whilst latterly, ETS has been at the forefront of computer-based testing (the now defunct TOEFL CBT and more recently internet-based testing (TOEFL IBT) introduced in 2006), the new IBT version no longer retains the computer adaptive functionality of its predecessor (Fulcher, 2009), although a new speaking component added in 2009 could be seen to compete with the new technologies of PTE Academic (Chung, 2009).

Hale, Stansfield and Duran (1984) catalogued TOEFL-related research which was produced between 1963 and 1982. More recently, ETS has displayed a series of downloadable TOEFL-related research reports on the internet. It should be remembered, however, that much of the enquiry which investigates TOEFL has actually been commissioned under ETS' own auspices. This inevitably leads to questions of objectivity regarding the breadth of enquiry which has been explored and the extent to which research outcomes with any potential negative marketing potential are made available for publication. Importantly, Chapman (2003, p. 1) cautions that the public has low trust in research undertaken by organizations that also design and market tests.

Whilst a connection between testing research and marketeering is in no way limited to ETS and TOEFL, Raimes (1990) also warns that ETS does strictly control the TOEFL research agenda. Concerns associated with this are further supported by Bachman, Lynch and Kunnan (1989, p. 223), who raised allegations of bias after reading a research paper written by Henning (1989) and commissioned by ETS. It should also be added, however, that such claims of bias are strongly denied by Connor (1992, pp. 177–178), who affirms, from experience, that the regulation of research data and the nature of studies is not a practice undertaken by ETS.

Task 3

- To what extent have you been aware of changes in approach to assessments like TOEFL?
- In your view, which developments in the TOEFL test do you feel have been most positive or important?
- What are your views on the ethicality of research which is commissioned by exam boards relating to their own assessments?
- What difficulties might emerge if a test of EAP is associated with a profit-making organization?

Lessons in EAP assessment from IELTS

The immediate precursor of IELTS, The English Language Testing Service (ELTS) was first delivered in 1980 when it succeeded the EPTB (IELTS, 2008). As explained by Weir (1983, p. 5), the structure and design of ELTS was inspired by communicative language learning and English for Specific Purposes (ESP). Research conducted by Caroll (in Alderson & Hughes, 1981) for the purpose of ELTS development, under contract to the British Council, sought to design a testing system with a sociolinguistic foundation, through the analysis of the communicative needs of international students. Consequently, five academic subject-related modules were created, in addition to a general academic module, with a view to servicing a range of different academic domains in higher education (Clapham, 1996; IELTS, 2008). At this point, central to ELTS was the premise that no single test could cater for the needs of all users (Weir, 1983, p. 5). This was consistent with contemporary research into ESP. Interestingly, this same theory was subsequently rejected by some of the same researchers who advocated the modular ESP approach including, in particular, Clapham (1996).

Task 4

- What is your stance on English for General Academic Purposes and English for Specific Academic Purposes?
- Do you feel that different subject areas require different tests of English for Academic Purposes? How does this relate to what has been discussed relating to construct validity in other chapters of this book?
- How easy is it to reflect the language constructs which relate to a complex academic discipline in a short test of EAP/EGAP/ESAP?
- What practical or resource-related issues might need to be considered with the development of different tests for different subject areas?

In 1986, Criper and Davies finished a four-year validation study of the ELTS test (see Alderson & Clapham, 1992, p. 152; Criper & Davies, 1988), which was commissioned due to concerns that ELTS was based on an 'outdated model' of language proficiency (Alderson & Clapham, 1992, p. 150). As a result, the test was then remodelled with the direction of Charles Alderson (see Alderson & Clapham, 1993; Charge & Taylor, 1997; IELTS, 2008).

According to Alderson and Clapham (1993, p. 1), the new revisions which were launched in 1989 represented a compromise between practicality and maximum predictive power. Consequently, the series of subject-specific modules, described by Williams (1988, p. 23) as a cosmetic attempt to cater for specialization, was reduced from six to four and a general training module was introduced. Although, in terms of face validity, the subject-specific modular approach was very popular amongst academics, it was considered that the different subject modules in the test were becoming increasingly difficult to define and delineate (Criper & Davies, 1988, p. 99).

Task 5

- In your view, to what extent should test practicality take precedence over construct validity, or vice versa?
- Does your department adopt an EGAP or an ESAP approach, or a combination of the two? What is your supporting rationale for your personal or departmental approach?
- Given the range of modules and specialism within academic disciplines, is it ever really possible to devise a test for a specific purpose which caters for the breadth of themes within that domain?

It can be inferred from the term 'practicality' that the resource implications associated with the maintenance of the bank of ELTS subject-specific modules was not considered sustainable for the future of ELTS. However, this does not necessarily mean that investment in the enhancement of their construct validity may not have resulted in a more appropriate solution for stakeholders of ELTS. As explained by Williams (1988, p. 24) and Davies (2008, p. 69), there is a conflict between economics and communicative testing.

It is also interesting to note that consideration of student needs analysis, a central theme of the research conducted by Weir (1983 and 1990), did not appear to have been so central to the redesign of ELTS. Interestingly, depending on standpoint, this could be considered simultaneously as either an improvement or erosion of construct validity, as it moves away from concern with specificity and domain in terms of content validity (Widdowson, 1983) and yet also places less emphasis on the abilities students need to acquire, as identified through empirical research, in favour of post hoc 'expert' support for the authenticity of newly revised ELTS test items (Weir, 1990, p. 21). After the revisions to ELTS were completed, the test was launched and the word 'International' was added in order to acknowledge the test's association with International Development Program Education Australia (now known as IDP) and to signal a commitment to a global outlook. The test then became known as IELTS.

Table 3 summarizes the evolution of IELTS. Again, practitioners involved in EAP assessment can follow and critique the changes which IELTS has undergone. An historical review of IELTS shows changing attitudes towards the construct of EAP proficiency.

Table 3: The history of IELTS (Davies, 2008; IELTS, 2012; Knapp, Seidlhofer & Widdowson, 2009, p. 631 and 637)

Test name/ Phase	Approach	Content
EPTB (Precursor of ELTS) (1960s onwards)	Structuralist approach	Focus on features of language and learners' challenges. Sampling undertaken of the linguistic features of lectures, textbooks and journal articles.
ELTS (1980)	Shift in the direction of a communicative approach.	Focus on ESP. Provision of texts for listening and written assessment from a series of supposed authentic domains.
IELTS (Since 1990s)	Movement away from language uses towards an approach favouring features of language use.	Changing focus from situations of subject-specific language use in academic contexts towards a more general and more abstract view of what constitutes academic discourse.
IELTS (Since 2005)	Computer-based IELTS is developed and trialled, although not yet fully launched.	

A frank critique of some of the potential shortfalls which can be associated with IELTS was presented in a radio broadcast by Ingram (2005), Australia's representative on the British–Australian research group that developed the IELTS Test and Australia's chief IELTS examiner for a period of ten years. These concerns are summarized below in Table 4 (ibid.).

Table 4: Ingram's concerns about the use and misuse of IELTS (Ingram, 2005)

Ingram's concern	Advice
IELTS is designed to be administered globally on a large scale. Consequently, the test's design had to make compromises to meet these administrative demands.	IELTS should not be considered a perfect measure. Proficiency levels set for university admission should be sufficiently generous to allow some level of variation from the actual levels specified in the students' results.
Many universities fail to require a proficiency level in IELTS sufficient to enable students to manage academic study without English hindering their performance.	The minimum required level for students entering academic programmes should be an overall band score of 7. If students are to be accepted at 6.5 or 6, they should be provided with ongoing English language support.

The results of an IELTS test provide a separate proficiency rating for speaking, listening, reading and writing. However, most universities simply use the overall band score for entry purposes.	Universities should look at each course and decide what level of proficiency in each skill students need to cope with the course activities.
IELTS is used for purposes for which it was not designed. In addition to university entry, IELTS is now also used for immigration purposes, to see whether an applicant for vocational registration has enough English to work, for example, as a teacher, a nurse or a tradesman.	Test misuse is highly unethical. A test should not be used for any purposes for which it was not developed.
There is evidence that some universities and admissions staff are willing to sacrifice both calibre of students and the quality of their courses for the income that international students offer.	Undergraduate students should not be accepted with a proficiency level below IELTS 7.0, especially if there is a failure to provide ongoing English language support.

Lessons in Assessment Literacy from PTE Academic

Pearson Test of English Academic (PTE Academic) is a relatively new computer-based international English language test introduced internationally in 2009 (Zheng & De Jong, 2011). Pearson is an international educational services company based in London. Pearson Test of English Academic was established as a result of a process of international field testing including more than 10,400 international students (PRWEB, 2009). Like IELTS and TOEFL, the purpose of PTE Academic is to assess English language competence for the purpose of admission to academic programmes where English language is the medium of delivery. Whilst it could be argued that, by the time of PTE Academic's introduction, the market for EAP assessment was already dominated by IELTS and TOEFL, Pearson saw a gap in the market for the use of technology in the process of delivery and assessment, with a view to enhancing reliability and a quicker turnaround of test results (Pearson, 2011). In PTE Academic, the speaking and writing test components are marked using Pearson's own patented automated scoring technologies. According to research commissioned by Pearson, the electronic marking which is integral to PTE Academic provides scores which are comparable to those provided by human markers, but with the reliability of a machine, thus enhancing reliability and validity. With the need to have a body of research behind the test, Pearson has already established a series of sponsored research papers which seek to demonstrate the robust nature of the test.

Task 6

- How comfortable are you with the concept of a test which is marked using computers rather than people?
- What are your views on the reliability of human markers compared to computerized marking systems?
- In your opinion, what are the relative strengths and weaknesses of humans and computers as EAP test assessors?
- Do you agree or disagree that EAP assessors might become deskilled if computerized marking becomes more prevalent?

Dr John de Jong, Vice President of Test Development at Pearson and Chair in Language Testing at Vrije Universiteit in Amsterdam (in Swain, 2012), supports the computerized systems which are used for testing purposes by referring to other examples of communication via computer technology in high-stakes contexts, such as the stock exchange, where computers are responsible for multi-million dollar transactions on a daily basis.

According to De Jong (in Swain, ibid.) the computer software used by Pearson has been programmed to compare students' responses with a database of tens of thousands of samples of language from academic contexts. During the marking process, the computers can compare thousands of texts that were written by candidates and rated by humans. It is claimed that the computers have already determined which characteristics the reference bank of essays were required to achieve in order to be awarded certain scores by human markers and then the same data is referenced to determine a mark for a new test taker. Human markers are still involved in marking procedures under circumstances of uncertainty, which is estimated to equate to approximately 4% of answers.

Despite successes, such as acceptance by UK Visas and Immigration (UKVI) for some study-visa issuance purposes, comments from admissions colleagues in the USA and academics in the UK (Table 5) at the time of the launch of PTE Academic exemplify the caution expressed at the prospect of this new examination on the EAP testing scene.

Table 5: Comments on the launch of PTE Academic (Chung, 2009; CollegeConfidential, 2009; Stewart, 2009; Swain, 2012)

Commentator	Summarized comment
Karen Kristof Senior Associate Director of Admission Smith College (USA) (Chung, 2009)	'We want to be flexible – but careful – in our English proficiency requirements.' Smith College has not yet decided whether it will accept PTE Academic scores. The college used to accept TOEFL exclusively and only very recently added IELTS. It is too soon to be able to comment on the efficacy of PTE Academic.
Glenn Fulcher Professor of Language Testing University of Leicester (UK) (Swain, 2012)	Computer scoring correlates just as highly with human scores as human scores do with each other; however, a human benchmark for computer validity weakens claims that machines will be more reliable. The critical consideration is whether marking criteria used by computers are comparable to those used by humans, which can identify richness and nuance in EAP skills.
Liz Hamp-Lyons, Professor of English Language Assessment University of Bedfordshire (UK) (Swain, 2012)	PTE offers busy admissions staff a rapid source of information about students' ability, but only a very restricted view of speaking ability is presented. A speaking test which is marked using automated scoring cannot substitute a human interview test.
Bethan Marshall Senior lecturer in English and Education King's College London (Stewart, 2009)	Computers are reliable as they will always assess in exactly the same way. But people write for people rather than computers. If a computer is marking tests, there is risk of backwash through writing for the computer.
Tim Oates Research director at Cambridge Assessment (Stewart, 2009)	It is extremely unlikely that automated scoring systems will not be used extensively in educational assessment in future. It is a question of 'when' not 'if'.

Task 7

- What is your current experience of computerized text and voice recognition systems and how do you feel these relate to new computerized assessment mechanisms for EAP?

- To what extent do you feel that the use of technology in assessment can lead to the deskilling of human markers in a similar way, as has happened in industrial contexts where machines have taken over the roles of humans?

- Do you feel that there are circumstances where computerized markers may be more consistent than human markers?

Challenges facing computerized testing mechanisms

An additional challenge facing computerized testing mechanisms may also stem from the fact that the general public may be unaware of key advancements in speech and writing assessment technologies, such as those described by Holland and Fisher (2008). As a result, there is a chance that certain individuals and institutions may continue to be sceptical of such technology (CollegeConfidential, 2009; Swain, 2012) due to negative experiences with low-quality telephone voice recognition systems and the inefficacy of computerized predictive text and online translation. In general, the reaction to automated scoring has been variable (Xi, 2010) from language testing academics and, at best, it can currently be described as cautiously optimistic.

One clear impact of automated scoring does appear to be the accuracy of test scores, particularly in speaking assessments, due to the removal of human unreliability. Carey, Mannell and Dunn (2011) discuss unreliability in IELTS speaking test marking. Nevertheless, it is also the case that the risks associated with automated scoring may also be due to the absence of the human thought process, which allows for the ability to assess a wider range of essential qualities of performance, the identification of cheating and the use of a broader series of tasks (Xi, 2012, p. 439). Parallels which highlight the strengths and weaknesses of automation, as described above, can also be drawn with manufacturing industries which have faced automation. In an account of what is described as a new industrial revolution associated with computer integrated manufacturing, Ayres (1991, p. 2) refers to the strengths of computers in terms of programmability, but, similarly, identifies shortfalls in flexibility.

Task 8

- Where do you stand on the use of technology in the marking of EAP assessments?
- Do you feel that electronic marking processes will become more commonplace over time? Where do you think the boundaries are between the efficacy of technology and the flexibility and professional experience of the human marker?

With regard to the future of Assessment Literacy associated with EAP, automated scoring offers the EAP sector additional challenges. If human beings are likely to be less involved with the process of language assessment for commercial tests, then a number of key opportunities for direct involvement in training for and critique of EAP assessment, on a broader scale and outside the confines of individual institutions or departments, will reduce. EAP practitioners will then potentially face a similar situation to the American manufacturing industries in the 1930s as a result of a form of EAP assessment *Fordism–Taylorism*, which may lead to deskilling due to the automation of the assessment processes (Wood, 1989, p. 3).

As a result of the considerations addressed above, in conjunction with three particular large-scale tests in EAP, the quest to develop skills in assessment requires the EAP practitioner to read between the lines so that an objective view of any EAP test's development and impact is not masked by other commercial factors and social implications. The companies behind tests such as IELTS, TOEFL and PTE Academic are fully aware that they are in close competition and, as a result, make every effort to market their assessments as extensively as possible. As this section has demonstrated, Assessment Literacy can gain from an understanding of both the innovations in test construct and delivery mechanisms, along with the associated social and political drivers which can be revealed on closer inspection.

Extension activities

The following extension activities can be exploited by colleagues who have additional time to explore and develop the strategies and principles introduced in this chapter.

» After following the areas of discussion in this chapter, consider the strong and weak points of a number of different standardized and commercially offered tests which relate to EAP. Reflect on how your understanding of these strengths and weaknesses has informed your approach to your own EAP assessment.

» If you haven't yet had time to act on what you have learnt from standardized EAP assessments, which areas of your EAP assessment practice do you feel should be targeted for enhancement, based on areas of good practice that you have noted?

» What are your views on the reliability and validity of commercial standardized EAP tests, compared with the reliability and validity of locally developed tests linked to EAP departments?

» In your view, in terms of what can be determined about a student's proficiency in EAP skills, how do externally available EAP tests compare with assessments undertaken through learning opportunities such as pre-sessional courses?

» What are the social and political implications of large-scale standardized tests? How are people's lives affected? Has teaching in your country institution been influenced by changes in UKVI procedures? Has this had a positive or negative impact on students and recruitment to your programmes or courses?

» As mentioned in this chapter, testing companies sometimes have to make compromises in their assessments, due to practicalities in test delivery. What do you think some of these compromises might involve?

Stakeholder support – 'Did you know …?'

Once you have applied the strategies and principles in this chapter to your EAP assessment context, the following information can be photocopied or adapted for use with different stakeholder groups, such as test takers, parents and staff, who are involved in or affected by your EAP testing and assessment. Consider how this passage could be modified or applied in your own working context.

PHOTOCOPIABLE

Did you know … that we recognize the benefits associated with experience of interpreting and understanding the features of standardized tests linked to EAP?

As experienced EAP practitioners, we recognize that skill in the development of EAP assessment is accrued over time through professional practice and understanding of the challenges which international students face in using EAP in higher education.

Whilst it is clear that working in teams with an EAP department to develop and mark local tests of EAP is a crucial part of many EAP teachers' roles, we also recognize that broader experience of the external tests which students use to gain admission to higher education can play an important role in EAP assessment-related continuing professional development.

Through gaining familiarity with externally provided tests, practitioners can encounter a range of different question items and approaches to assessment, which can both inspire innovation or identify areas to avoid in local contexts.

EAP teachers who have experience of working as examiners for external testing boards can gain transferable experience of alternative assessment criteria and procedures designed to enhance the reliability of marking and moderation, which have been developed and trialled extensively by companies with large research budgets.

In addition to gaining experience which can inform local assessment design, a good knowledge of external examinations also allows us to support colleagues working in admissions across the institutions in which we work.

References

Alderson, J. C., & Clapham, C. (1992). Applied linguistics and language testing: A case study of the ELTS test. *Applied Linguistics, 13*(2), 149–167.

Alderson, J. C., & Clapham, C., (Eds.). (1992). *Examining the ELTS test: An account of the first stage of the ELTS revision project*. Research report No. 2. London; Cambridge; Canberra: The British Council; University of Cambridge Local Examination Syndicate; IDP Australia.

Alderson, J. C., & Hamp-Lyons, L., (1996). TOEFL preparation courses: A study of washback. *Language Testing, 13*(3), 2800–2897.

Alderson, J. C., & Hughes, A. (1981). *Issues in language testing*. London: British Council.

Ayres, R. U. (1991). *Computer integrated manufacturing*. London: Chapman and Hall.

Bachman, L. F., Lynch, B., & Kunnan, A. (1989). Response to Henning. *Language Testing, 6*(2), 223–229. doi:10.1177/026553228900600208

Blue, G. M., Milton, J., & Saville, J. (2000). *Assessing English for academic purposes*. Oxford; New York: P. Lang.

Carey, M. D., Mannell, R. H., & Dunn, P. K. (2011). Does a rater's familiarity with a candidate's pronunciation affect the rating in oral proficiency interviews? *Language Testing, 28*(2), 201–219.

Carroll, B. J. (1981). Specifications for an English language testing service. In J. C. Alderson & A. Hughes (Eds.), *Issues in language testing*. Oxford: Pergamon Press.

Chapman, M. (2003). TOEIC: Tried but undertested. *Shiken: JALT Testing & Evaluation SIG Newsletter, 7*(3), 2–5.

Charge, N., & Taylor, L. B. (1997). Recent developments in IELTS. *ELT J, 51*(4), 374–380. doi:10.1093/elt/51.4.374

Chung, J. (2009, October 6). Pearson plans to release English proficiency exam to rival TOEFL. *The Daily Pennsylvanian*. Retrieved from http://www.thedp.com/article/2009/10/pearson_plans_to_release_english_proficiency_exam_to_rival_toefl

Clapham, C. (1996). *The development of IELTS: A study of the effect of background knowledge on reading comprehension*. Cambridge: Cambridge University Press.

CollegeConfidential (2009). *New English language test challenges TOEFL*. USA Education Guides. Retrieved from http://www.collegeconfidential.com/new-english-language-test-challenges-toefl/

Connor, U. (1992). Two commentaries on Ann Raimes's "The TOEFL test of written English: Causes for concern". A reader reacts. *TESOL Quarterly, 26*(1), 177–179.

Criper, C., & Davies, A. (1988). *ELTS validation project* (Research report). London, Cambridge: The British Council, University of Cambridge Local Examination Syndicate.

Davies, A. (2008). *Assessing academic English: Testing English proficiency, 1950–1989 – the IELTS solution.* Cambridge: Cambridge University Press.

Davies, A., Brown A., Elder, C., Hill, K., Lumley, T., & McNamara, T. (1999). *Dictionary of language testing.* Cambridge: Cambridge University Press.

ETS. (2011). *TOEFL program history* (TOEFL iBT Research Insight, Series 1, Volume 6).

Foucault, M. (1991). *Discipline and punish: The birth of the prison.* London: Penguin.

Fulcher, G. (2009). *Language testing for higher education.* Retrieved from http://languagetesting.info/whatis/scenarios/4hedu.php

Hale, G. A., Stansfield, C. W., & Duran, R. P. (1984). A comprehensive TOEFL bibliography, 1963–82. *The Modern Language Journal, 68*(1), 45.

Henning, G. (1989). Comments on the comparability of TOEFL and Cambridge CPE. *Language Testing, 6*(2), 217–222.

Holland, V. M., & Fisher, F. P. (2008). *The path of speech technologies in computer assisted language learning: From research toward practice.* New York; London: Routledge.

Hughes, A. (1988). *Testing English for university study.* Oxford: Modern English Publications in association with the British Council.

Hughes, A. (2003). *Testing for language teachers* (2nd ed.). Cambridge: Cambridge University Press.

IELTS. (2008). *IELTS history.* Retrieved from http://www.ielts.org/aboutus/article284.aspx

IELTS. (2012). *The history of IELTS.* Retrieved from http://www.ielts.org/researchers/history_of_ielts.aspx

Ingram, D. (2005). *English language problems in Australian universities* [Radio broadcast]. Lingua Franca.

Knapp, K., Seidlhofer, B., & Widdowson, H. G. (2009). *Handbook of foreign language communication and learning.* New York: Mouton de Gruyter.

McNamara, T. F. (1996). *Measuring second lanaguage performance.* London: Longman.

McNamara, T. F. (2000). *Language testing.* Oxford: Oxford University Press.

Pearson. (2012). *Automated Scoring*. Retrieved from http://pearsonpte.com/research/Pages/AutomatedScoring.aspx

PRWEB (Producer). (2009, September 8). *Pearson launches new global test of English*. Retrieved from http://www.prweb.com/releases/2009/09/prweb2835434.htm

Raimes, A. (1990). The TOEFL test of written English: Causes for concern. *TESOL Quarterly, 24*(3), 427–442.

Shohamy, E. (2001). *The power of tests: A critical perspective on the uses of language tests*. Harlow: Longman.

Spolsky, B. (1995). Measured words: The development of objective language testing. *Applied Linguistics, 17*(4), 544–547.

Stewart, W. (2009). Essays to be marked by 'robots'. *TES Newspaper*. Retrieved from http://www.tes.co.uk/article.aspx?storycode=6023725

Swain, H. (2012, May 7). Patrick McGhee, new chair of Million+ thinktank, is trending nationally. *The Guardian*. Retrieved from http://www.theguardian.com/education/2012/may/07/patrick-mcghee-chair-millionplus-thinktank

Taylor, C., & Angelis, P. (2008). The evolution of TOEFL. In C. Chapelle, M. Enright & J. Jamieson (Eds.), *Building a validity argument for the Test of English as a Foreign Language* (pp. 27–54). New York; London: Routledge.

Weir, C. J. (1983). *Identifying the language problems of overseas students in tertiary education in the United Kingdom* (PhD Thesis). University of London Institute of Education.

Weir, C. J. (1990). *Communicative language testing*. New York: Prentice Hall.

Widdowson, H. G. (1983). *Learning purpose and language use*. Oxford: Oxford University Press.

Williams, E. (1988). Comments and reaction to ELTS revision (Unpublished archive document). *The Modern Language Journal, 67*(1), 41–55.

Wood, S. (1989). *The transformation of work?: Skill, flexibility and the labour process*. London: Unwin Hyman.

Xi, X. (2010). Automated scoring and feedback systems: Where are we and where are we heading? *Language Testing, 27*(3), 291–300.

Xi, X. (2012). Validity and the automated scoring of performance tests. In F. Davidson & G. Fulcher (Eds.), *The Routledge handbook of language testing* (pp. 438–451). Oxford: Routledge.

Zheng, Y., & De Jong, J. H. A. L. (2011). *Establishing construct and concurrent validity of Pearson test of English academic* (Research Summaries and Notes). Retrieved from http://pearsonpte.com/research/Documents/RN_EstablishingConstructAndConcurrentValidityOfPTEAcademic_2011.pdf

Chapter 15: EAP assessment voices

This chapter will:
- provide a range of views based on the experiences of EAP practitioners who are involved with assessment.
- encourage critical reflection on the EAP assessment practice of others.
- stimulate the implementation of actions for personal practice based on review of the EAP assessment experience of others.

You will have the opportunity to:
- read more about the challenges which EAP assessment practitioners have encountered in their work.
- use another reflective learning tool to instigate action for the enhancement of EAP assessment practice.

Reflection on the views of EAP practitioners

The theory and conceptual frameworks offered by published research into language assessment are key to improving skills in EAP assessment. However, the hands-on experiences of practitioners who are working practically in the field of EAP (Manning, 2013) can also provide a great deal of information and assistance to colleagues who are seeking to learn from good practice and avoid common pitfalls.

Consequently, this chapter presents a series of practitioner views surrounding certain key themes which have been addressed in this book. The reader is then invited to reflect on the views expressed, in order to consider how they relate to his or her own EAP assessment practice and to encourage action based on critical reflection of assessment practice.

For each bank of EAP assessment voices, readers are encouraged to use a process such as Kolb's Learning/Reflective Cycle, another mechanism to work towards meaningful outcomes as part of reflective learning. In Chapter 6, we already used an applied model called Gibb's Cycle for a similar purpose.

In Kolb's view (1975, 1984), each of the stages of the learning/reflective cycle play a key function. In the initial stage, *Concrete Experience* has a special focus on identifying scenarios and relating to experiences, including those of others, so that learning can be engendered with other people. As part of the *Reflective Observation* element, the participant drives their learning through observing the situation in detail and considering multiple perspectives. *Abstract Conceptualization* then involves the drawing of conclusions and the application of logic, in contrast to feelings. Finally, through *Active Experimentation*, theories can be applied or tested with a view to making a change or a positive impact or outcome.

The stages of Kolb's Cycle are shown below in a model adapted for the context of EAP assessment, which includes a series of guiding questions related to EAP assessment. Completing this reflection should result in tangible action points for the enhancement of EAP assessment practice in your own context or that of your wider EAP assessment team.

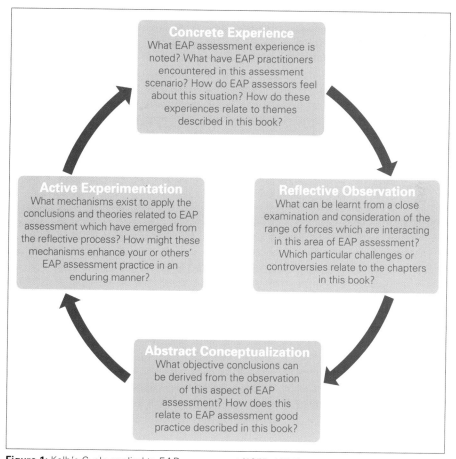

Figure 1: Kolb's Cycle applied to EAP assessment (1975, 1984)

EAP assessment voices: Designing and creating tests

We haven't really followed a procedure for the design of EAP assessments. I think that's where we have fallen down in the past. Although, you know, we've never had problems or particular criticisms from our external examiners. I suppose there's no formal procedure that we follow when we put a test or assessment together. We do try to sit around the table and work out what we're planning to do and how we are going to test the students. I'd really like to get a more structured process in place so that we have a more definite approach in future.

Honestly, our approach to EAP test design is just based on looking at previous years' EAP tests. We take time to think about which areas of the test worked well and which didn't work so well last time. We also take into account what we've already achieved in our scheme of work and learning outcomes. This is usually the baseline.

Well, in my view, the assessment design is part of the course design. In my mind, they go together. In most cases, for the EAP assessment that I'm involved with, I find that the assessment requirements are more or less defined by the link academic department. In that kind of situation, I like to sit down with academics from the relevant school. I try to draw texts from their reading lists and identify what the linguistic features of those texts are. But, then, in the institutes that I have worked in, these ideals don't always coincide with reality.

EAP assessment voices: Validity and reliability

I have to admit that we don't do a lot of work on validity and reliability. I think we tend to just choose texts from what we think are serious academic sources which are related to academic studies in some way. And often, sadly, I think we tend to dumb down the content by choosing newspaper articles when we should be looking for suitable academic texts, which we just don't have the time to do.

We haven't really followed a procedure for the design of EAP assessments. I think that's where we have fallen down in the past. Although, you know, we've never had problems or particular criticisms from our external examiners. I suppose there's no formal procedure that we follow when we put a test or assessment together. We do try to sit around the table and work out what we're planning to do and how we are going to test the students. I'd really like to get a more structured process in place so that we have a more definite approach in future.

I mean I suppose I could say, just to start with, that there is tension between assessing the language and skills that you need in EAP, versus trying to adhere to good standards of reliability. In other words, you know, to ensure reliable assessment, you'll be more likely to get a reliable assessment, statistically speaking, if you use a test which requires objective answers like multiple-choice or one-word answers. But then, if you try to use that approach of testing, you'll probably end up not really assessing the kinds of skills that you want to assess. So, in order to assess the sort of skills like note-taking, summarizing, that kind of thing, which is more appropriate in an EAP context because you are preparing students to go on to use those skills on their degree courses, then you'll end up with types of assessment which are more subjective and less reliable from the marking point of view.

EAP assessment voices: Professional strengths and weaknesses in EAP assessment

I think my main weakness in terms of EAP assessment is that I tend to accept that the approach followed by common standardized tests is the right approach when, in fact, it may not always be the right way of doing things. My strength perhaps is that I'm increasingly questioning the way that we do EAP assessment, and what I'm really interested in is breaking down the barriers between test papers, for example, of the reading and the writing into two completely separate tests.

I don't think I have fully worked out a coherent conception of what I'm aiming to do with EAP testing, how it all fits into an integrated whole. And I think that's partly because of disagreements that I have seen in the wider field, or perhaps just with the people that I have been exposed to. There seems to me to be some disagreement, both in terms of the importance of aspects of assessment such as formative, genre types, use of discrete items and language knowledge.

I think I'm reasonably good at producing test materials because I have some experience in producing commercial teaching materials for publication. I think that you need to be able to produce high-quality materials for testing, as well as for teaching and published materials. So, I do think that I am reasonably good in that area. I am confident that I know how to analyze test results to some extent, but there are certain statistical techniques that I don't know much about. I can do the basics like item analysis and internal reliability and that kind of thing. I think the crunch area for me actually is turning scores into something which is reportable, and I suspect that this is an area of weakness for many teachers involved in EAP assessment.

EAP assessment voices: Training in EAP assessment

Although I haven't had a lot of training, I'm aware of how complex EAP assessment is and how important it is. You just have to get the level right and you have to assess what you've taught. So, I'm aware of the issues and if I don't quite know how to do it, I have a sense that I should find out or should ask a colleague for help. Logistically, the biggest challenge is continuing to recreate assessments, because you need new assessments each year or sometimes each term.

In my MA in Applied Linguistics, I took a Testing course. That's what I did at the beginning. And then I taught on a pre-sessional course. When I did that, I learnt a lot because the course director was also a testing teacher. So, I also developed a lot of skills related to EAP assessment through being involved with the marking and moderation process for pre-sessional EAP tests and through my more general experience of grading standardized external tests through exam boards. I'm also still teaching academic English and designing tests to see whether our students meet the requirements of the schools where they will be studying for their degrees.

I think I have learnt most through trial and error and through working with more experienced colleagues. I think there's very little formal professional developmental in EAP and I think at some places I've worked, there's not a great deal of agreement with some of the fundamentals. So, I think it's been through work with course leaders who have shared their thoughts, and then experimenting with things like wanting to try it myself. I think what BALEAP are doing with EAP teacher competencies is very interesting.

EAP assessment voices: Marking and interpreting test scores

Now we've got a set of criteria that we have to use for assessment purposes and these are institutional criteria that have been pre-set by our faculty. I think they're pretty carefully thought-out criteria, so I put a lot of trust in them. Occasionally, I wonder if, for certain discrete items, I might need something a bit different. But I do think it's much better than the days when we just used our professional experience without a benchmark to refer to.

 I don't feel at all confident that my EAP test grades are completely accurate, but I do try to practise a form of moderation and I do look back at the test papers that are way out of sync with others in my class and I ask myself if I have done something wrong. Recently, there was a question that just two students got right and I thought, well, that's obviously ambiguous and what people said was not what I wanted, although I had thought it was a suitable question before I first ran the test.

I don't regard myself as a very competent or consistent marker. I try to be, but I ... I think lots of English teachers can tell what their students want to say, and that is not what you're supposed to do when you're supposedly marking objectively. So I have to continually stop myself from doing that. I think also because I have taught a lot of students from one particular nationality, I have started not to notice some of the common errors that they make. I sometimes have to double-check my marking because of that.

EAP assessment voices: Concerns about EAP assessment

 I think that consistency is a big problem. I do see students here in Australia at our university occasionally and I think there's no way they've got whatever grade they claim to have got and I know it's really difficult to keep it exact, but I do know that students sometimes manage to slip through and that test results seem to be affected by which country the test has been taken in. You also sometimes fear that something corrupt may have happened in some cases and that the student has managed to get a score that they didn't actually deserve. In some cases, I fear that the student in front of me didn't really do the test that they have presented or, worse still, that somebody else did it. I'm sure these things happen quite a lot in quite a few countries.

I have noticed some pre-sessional courses focus too much on assessment, rather than on developing students' key EAP skills. I really think that this approach risks disadvantaging some groups of students as opposed to other people going into the system who either already have that EAP knowledge or just had better training.

 Well, I think I mentioned I'm always worried about larger-scale standardized tests. It definitely worries me that they are turning into an EAP assessment machine. And especially when I was working in China, you could just see the sheer volume; you don't get the same idea in Britain at all. Thousands of students were obsessed with doing EAP tests every month, so ... I mean just to put you a bit in the picture, let's say every month in the region that I lived in, there were nine exam centres delivering three to four tests. I didn't want to even think about all the time and effort being invested into students cramming for these tests. They were starting to take over people's lives.

References

Gibbs, G. (1988). *Learning by doing: A guide to teaching and learning methods*. London: Further Education Unit.

Kolb, D. A. (1984). *Experiential learning. Experience as the source of learning and development*. Englewood Cliffs, New Jersey: Prentice Hall.

Kolb, D. A., & Fry, R. (1975). Toward an applied theory of experiential learning. In C. Cooper (Ed.), *Theories of group process*. London: Wiley.

Manning, A. (2013). *EAP teacher assessment literacy* (Ed.D. thesis). Leceister: University of Leicester.

Chapter 15: EAP assessment voices

Glossary

Chapter 1

Achievement (test/assessment)
EAP assessments of this nature are used to determine if students have achieved EAP learning outcomes appropriate for particular grades or levels. They could also be used to measure the effectiveness of teachers and institutions in assisting EAP students to achieve intended learning outcomes.

Criterion-referenced (test/assessment)
EAP tests which assess EAP students' achievement through comparing learning outcomes achieved with pre-defined assessment criteria. Such criteria are intended to represent the skills required in a general or specific academic domain.

Diagnostic (test/assessment)
This type of EAP assessment is used to identify students' particular EAP learning requirements.

Direct (test/assessment)
The testing of EAP skills in an authentic context, such as the assessment of an academic seminar through observing and assessing seminar participation.

Discrete-point (test/assessment)
EAP tests which have been created to assess or measure more restricted or isolated EAP skills, such as the use of connective devices or the passive voice.

Formative assessment
An EAP assessment which focuses on the improvement of learning and the provision of actionable feedback.

Indirect (test/assessment)
Less organic mechanisms for the assessment of EAP skills, such as the use of cloze or multiple-choice questions.

Integrative (test/assessment)
EAP tests which have been devised in order to assess a series of EAP skills concurrently. This could involve integrated academic reading and writing tests which combine the assessment of research skills and the use of information gleaned from research in academic writing concurrently.

Marking criteria
A set of academic benchmarks used by all markers to attempt to position the EAP performance of candidates along a continuum of ability. With in-house proficiency or achievement assessments, marking criteria will ideally be linked to intended learning outcomes, and these will be made known to students and staff. It is also good practice for staff to have training in the interpretation of grading criteria.

Norm-referenced (test/assessment)
This kind of EAP test is less common, but could be used for the placement or streaming of EAP students into two or more groups. Relative achievement of students through the EAP test could determine which class the student is placed into.

Objective (test/assessment)
This involves comparing EAP test responses with a series of suitable responses, as designated in a key or list of answers.

Placement (test/assessment)
EAP assessments of this nature can be used to determine which students will be selected for a particular level of course or study.

Power (test/assessment)
Sufficient time is given to EAP test takers in order to complete the test. However, the items which are used in the test include a number of complex or difficult EAP challenges and consequently not all candidates are likely to be able to respond to each question appropriately or adequately.

Pre-sessional

An EAP course or programme which has been designed to develop the skills of students whose language proficiency does not yet meet the minimum requirements of university programmes. Typically, pre-sessional courses take place immediately prior to the start of the degree programmes which students are aiming to join.

Proficiency (test/assessment)

In this form of EAP assessment, a student's level of skill in a certain area as determined through a test to measure that skill.

Selection

These EAP tests or examinations are used to determine who will be selected to attend university, or they can also be used to place students in a particular class level. Tests of this nature can also be used to determine whether students require more or less intensive EAP study, or particular EAP modules.

Speed (test/assessment)

This type of approach could be utilized with a bank of multiple-choice or 'True or False' questions. Typically, the set of EAP items provided is sufficiently easy so that every student could theoretically answer all items correctly if there was sufficient time available. However, candidates are purposely not given sufficient time and, therefore, students' knowledge and speed of performance are tested.

Streaming

The placement of students into different classes according to current EAP skill ability.

Subjective (test/assessment)

The awarding of grades or marks for an EAP test through professional judgement.

Summative assessment

A summative EAP test is typically one that is used in order to calculate a mark which is used to demonstrate a student's proficiency or attainment. Students may then be measured, allowed to progress or blocked from entry depending on the level of the grade.

Support of learning

This form of EAP assessment is used to monitor the progress of learning; to provide learners with feedback on their learning, to help them improve; to assist teachers in identifying changes to be made in their EAP teaching; to enhance student motivation and confidence by demonstrating progress in EAP skill.

Test purpose

An EAP test's assessment objectives. It is necessary to determine these so that the right test can be chosen for particular circumstances.

Chapter 2

Construct
An area of ability or skill in EAP which is identified for operationalization within an EAP test.

Construct validity
The meaningfulness and appropriateness of the interpretations that we make on the basis of test scores. Wigdor and Garner's definition of construct validity (1982) describes construct validity as '… a scientific dialogue about the degree to which an inference that a test measures an underlying trait or hypothesized construct is supported by logical analysis and empirical evidence' (p. 62).

Content validity
The estimate of how much a measure accurately represents the different aspects of a construct in the authentic EAP subject domain or context on which the students' EAP teaching, learning and assessment is focused.

Criterion validity
The degree to which an EAP test accurately represents the EAP abilities or skills which it intends to measure.

Face validity
The level to which stakeholders agree or accept that a particular EAP test is a representative or useful measure of the EAP skills or abilities which it claims to measure.

Operationalize (a construct)
The manner in which an EAP skill area is manifested in a test item or question.

Reliability
Consistency of measurement and avoidance of variation in test scores due to factors other than the construct being measured.

Validity
A general term to describe the extent to which a test or assessment's results are representative of what that assessment seeks to measure.

Chapter 3

Field testing
The process through which possible EAP test items are reviewed and verified as suitable by being used in conditions which are sufficiently similar to those in which the final test will be deployed.

General description
An area within an example specification framework which provides a brief general statement of the behaviour being assessed. This is similar to learning outcomes or objectives.

Prompt attributes
An area within an example specification framework which provides a detailed description of what the student or test taker will encounter in this test item.

Prototyping and piloting
Part of the process of field testing, whereby potential EAP test items are identified as suitable for use in operational tests.

Response attributes
An area within an example specification framework which provides a complete and detailed description of the way in which the student will provide the answer and what will constitute success or failure.

Sample item
An example item or task that reflects the specification.

Specification supplement
A detailed explanation of any additional required information that is needed in order to create suitable items.

Test specification
A blueprint document through which alternative versions of an EAP test can be created.

Chapter 4

Deficiency analysis

This approach relates existing proficiency to target learner proficiency and identifies weaknesses or deficiencies and determines priorities.

Domain

The academic or subject field which represents the context in which EAP skills are to be used or developed.

English for General Academic Purposes (EGAP)

An approach to EAP which focuses on the development use or assessment of English in a broad academic context which aims to be transferable to any academic field.

English for Specific Academic Purposes (ESAP)

An approach to EAP which focuses on the development use or assessment of English linked to specific academic subjects or domains.

(Intended) Learning outcomes

A set of attainment benchmarks which represent the target learning objectives which students will realize through a course of EAP study.

Means analysis

Investigates the local teaching situation including facilities, teachers and teaching methods to see how the EAP course can be implemented.

Needs analysis

A process through which student and learning needs are investigated or evaluated, with the aim of identifying approaches for future learning and strengths and weaknesses.

Present-situation analysis

This approach focuses on learners' competence regarding skills and language at the beginning of the EAP course.

Sampling

The act of accurately identifying and drawing examples or constructs from the target academic domain(s).

Sampling variability

A phenomenon which transpires due to the difficulty in identifying constructs which are characteristic of, or essential to, a particular domain.

Specificity

The extent to which EAP assessment or teaching reflects the constructs which are particular to the academic domain in focus.

Strategy analysis

This approach focuses on methods of learning the required EAP skills. Learning style refers to the student's preferred way of learning.

Target situation analysis

A focus on learners' needs at the end of an EAP course and the benchmark of target-level performance.

Chapter 5

Alpha testing
A stage of pre-testing where individuals (experts or representative students) and small groups provide qualitative feedback on an EAP test regarding potential problems, specific tasks and instructions.

Beta testing
The collection of more quantitative feedback on an EAP test from larger groups of representative students or expert colleagues.

Critical social theory
An approach to assessment which considers the social and ideological forces and institutions which produce it and, potentially, constrain it.

Ethics
Alignment with the accepted principles of right and wrong in the EAP profession.

Gate-keeping
The function of an assessment when the level of score obtained by a test taker is linked to entry or exclusion from a higher level of study.

High-stakes
Related to the gate-keeping function of larger scale standardized tests, the results of which can have important repercussions on people's lives.

Postmodern(ism)
In the EAP context, postmodernism manifests itself through concerns linked to the interplay between information-seeking and power relations. Such concerns are particularly evident in the work of Shohamy (1998, 2001) and Benesch (2001, p. 60).

Stakeholder
An individual whose life, study or, ultimately, work, may be affected in some way by the results obtained by themselves or others in an EAP test.

Chapter 6

'Butler's stance'
The classification and potential subordination of EAP practitioners as 'support' staff (Raimes, 1991).

Hypothesis
A proposition which is subject to corroboration in order to determine if it can be accepted or refuted.

Null hypothesis
The opposite situation to the hypothesis. If support is found for the hypothesis, then the null hypothesis can be rejected.

Reflective practitioner
A practitioner who combines classroom practice experience with research (Wallace, 1991).

Test facet
An aspect of a performance or situation which can have an impact on EAP test results.

Chapter 7

Assessment for learning

An approach to EAP assessment where student learning is at the heart of an integrated approach to assessment. In this approach, high quality and appropriate assessment is a prerequisite for better student learning (Knight, 1995).

Calibrate

The act of testing assessment scales and undertaking training with the use of samples of performance and the intended scale, so that scales can be adjusted and markers can build consensus on valid and reliable usage.

The Common European Framework of Reference for Languages (CEFR)

A European, and increasingly international, mechanism to determine transferable language proficiency thresholds without the need to refer to the scales or criteria pertaining to particular commercial testing systems (see Council of Europe, 2007).

Scale

A set of criteria or EAP performance benchmarks which are used to determine the level of a test taker's performance.

Target Language Use (TLU)

See *Domain*.

Chapter 8

Corpus

A large set of texts which is usually stored electronically.

Flesch–Kincaid

An electronic mechanism to evaluate a text and allocate a numerical scale to categorize the text's readability level.

Rubric

Instructions to test takers within a test or test item.

(Test/Assessment) Authenticity

The degree of correspondence of the characteristics of a given language test task to the characteristics of a target language use task.

Note: The definition of *authenticity* varies according to different stakeholders.

(Test/Assessment) Impact

The various ways in which the EAP test use affects society.

(Test/Assessment) Interactivity

The extent to which the constructs we want to test are critically involved in accompanying the EAP test task.

(Test/Assessment) Practicality

The ways in which the EAP test will be implemented in a given situation or whether, in fact, the test will be used at all.

Chapter 9

Bimodal distribution
A polygon with two peaks.

Box and whisker (plot)
A means of representing the distribution of EAP test scores.

Descriptive statistics
Statistical procedures which are useful for identifying groupings or distributions within a set of data.

Interquartile range
Interquartile range is the range of the central half of a set of data. When compared to the range, the interquartile range is a more effective measure of central tendency, as it focuses on the spread of the middle half of the values.

Interval scale
Provides categories and ordering, and shows distance between points in that ordering. Notably, intervals have the same interpretation throughout (no absolute zero).

Kurtosis
The level of peakedness in symmetrical distributions in a frequency polygon.

Leptokurtic
A highly peaked polygon in a frequency polygon.

Mean
The average of a test score, often interpreted as an indicator of test difficulty or how a given group of students has performed.

Median
The midpoint value in a series of data and splits the data into two equal sets.

Mesokurtic
A middle peaked polygon (typical of normal distribution).

Mode
The mode is the most frequently occurring score.

Negatively skewed
A longer tail at the lower end and a peak at the upper end of the polygon.

Nominal scale
Provides names and categories only (no order implied).

Normal distribution
Used to describe a frequency polygon, takes the form of a bell curve. Normal distributions, which can vary in shape, appear in many naturally occurring situations, including in educational variables relevant to EAP, such as ability in different language skills.

Ordinal scale
Provides categories, but also provides the ordering or ranking of those categories (no information about distance between categories).

Platykurtic
A relatively flat polygon.

Positively skewed
A longer tail at the upper end and a peak at the lower end of the polygon.

Range
The range shows the difference between the highest and lowest scores. It can be calculated by subtracting the lowest score from the highest score.

Ratio scale
Provides the intervals between points in the ordering of certain categories, but with more information because there is an interpretable zero and multiples of points along the scale make sense.

Semi-interquartile range
The semi-interquartile range is the interquartile range divided by two $(Q3 - Q1) \div 2$. It is a measure of variability which is frequently used for data sets which are not normally distributed.

Skewness
A term used to refer to distributions which show a form of asymmetry.

Standard deviation
The standard deviation shows how much, on average, test scores vary or deviate from the mean.

Chapter 10

Correlation coefficients
Statistics calculated from data which summarize the strength and direction of the relationship between two variables.

Expert raters
In this process, raters are skilled practitioners in EAP, whose expert judgement is used to quantify the suitability of test content, often using rating scales. Typically, raters can be asked to annotate EAP tests or test items.

Factor analysis
This procedure can involve analysis of patterns in test scores of test takers who have taken a number of different test versions. In brief, the procedure allows responses to similar items which test the same construct to be conflated as a more powerful measure.

Inferential statistics
Statistical procedures which go beyond descriptive alternatives and which are more indicative of how analysis can relate to larger groups of people.

Internal reliability measures
Procedures used to interrogate internal consistency within a test and reliability of items and sections. Examples include: split half estimates (Guttman/Spearman-Brown); estimates based on item variances (Cronbach's Alpha); test-retest reliability estimates – also known as stability tests.

Item difficulty statistics
Statistics such as the Item difficulty index, Item discrimination index and Item-total test score correlations. These procedures are commonly used to: give feedback to test takers, teachers and test developers; help identify problems with items; identify weaknesses for correction; ascertain why items are not operating satisfactorily.

Marking reliability measures
This describes analyses which are used to investigate reliability of procedures associated with marking and awarding grades. These can include: Rater (Marker) reliability estimates; Phi coefficient dependability to measure the dependability of an EAP test score as a measure of mastery in a skill; and Agreement indices to measure the reliability of different bands or classifications related to mastery or non-mastery of EAP skills.

Pearson product-moment correlation coefficient
This technique requires the relationship between the two variables to be linear; both variables should constitute interval scales and both should be normally distributed.

Rasch analysis
Rasch Analysis offers evidence with regard to the extent to which a particular EAP item may under- or over-discriminate in relation to the overall total test score.

Spearman rank correlation
This technique can be used to investigate the relationship between two variables without interval measures or normal distribution.

T-tests and Analysis of Variance (ANOVA)
These procedures are commonly used to identify differences between two or more different groups of test score or class performance, based on different variables such as teaching methodology.

Verbal protocols
This technique involves the analysis of test-taker experiences, which are given verbally after a test has been taken.

Chapter 11

Domain underrepresentation
This situation arises as the skills that are necessary to pass an examination or assessment may not always be a comprehensive reflection of the target language use domain.

Standardized test/assessment
A standardized test is rigorously developed, uses standard procedures for administration and scoring, and has standard content. The term is often used to refer to large-scale testing ventures.

Washback
Washback usually refers to the impact which tests have on teaching professionals, test takers and educational environments. It is also frequently described as 'the tail wagging the dog' when tests influence a syllabus or teaching approach, rather than the other way around.

Chapter 12

Beneficence (The Principle of)
'The Principle of Beneficence' states that a test ought to bring about good in society.

EALTA
European Association for Language Testing and Assessment

ILTA
International Language Testing Association

Chapter 13

Assessment Literacy
The knowledge, skill and ability of educators, test takers and other stakeholders in the process of designing assessments (where applicable) and understating the results which they deliver.

Chapter 14

IELTS
International English Language Testing System

PTE Academic
Pearson Test of English Academic

TOEFL
Test of English as a Foreign Language

Chapter 15

Kolb's Cycle
A mechanism used to work towards meaningful outcomes as part of reflective learning. It is a four-stage learning cycle.
- Concrete Experience: Identifying and having an experience.
- Reflective Observation: Reflecting on the experience.
- Abstract Conceptualization: Drawing conclusions and learning from the experience.
- Active Experimentation: Applying what has been learnt.

Acknowledgements

Pages 3–4   Table 1: Functions of assessment, adapted from Berry, R. (2008). *Assessment for Learning*. Published by and reproduced with kind permission of Hong Kong University Press.

Page 5   Figure 1: The purpose of EAP assessment, extended and adapted from Alexander, O., Argent, S., & Spencer, J. (2008). *EAP Essentials: A Teacher's Guide to Principles and Practice*. Published by and reproduced with kind permission of Garnet Publishing Ltd.

Page 15   Text reproduced from Wigdor, A. K., & Garner, W.R. (1982). Ability testing: uses, consequences and controversies. *National Academy Press, 1*(3), 6–8. http://onlinelibrary.wiley.com/ doi/10.1111/j.1745-3992.1982.tb00659.x/. Reproduced with kind permission of Wiley Online Library.

Page 19   Table 2: Initial probing questions in the process of EAP construct validation, adapted from Messick, S. (1989). Validity. In R. L. Linn (Ed.), *Educational measurement* (3rd Edition) (pp. 13–103). New York: American Council on Education/Macmillan. Reproduced with kind permission of Rowman and Littlefield, https://ssl.acenet.edu/ contact-us/Pages/default.aspx.

Page 25   Figure 1: An EAP test design cycle with examples of information contributing to an EAP test specification, from *Practical Language Testing, Fulcher, G.,* Copyright © 2010 Hodder Education. Reproduced by permission of Taylor & Francis Books UK.

Pages 27–29   Table 1: EAP test specification format, adapted from Davidson, F., & Lynch, B. K. (2002). *Testcraft: a teacher's guide to writing and using language test specifications*. Published by and reproduced with kind permission of Yale University Press.

Page 30   Text reproduced from Fulcher, G., & Davidson, F. (2007). *Language testing and assessment: an advanced resource book*. Published by and reproduced with kind permission of Routledge.

Page 30   Text reproduced from Bachman, L. F. (2000). *Modern language testing at the turn of the century: assuring that what we want counts*. Language Testing, *17*(1), 1–42. Reproduced with kind permission of Sage Publications, http://ltj.sagepub.com/content/17/1/1.abstract.

Page 39   Figure 1: The course design balancing act, reproduced from Jordan, R. R. (1997). *English for academic purposes: A guide and resource book for teachers*. Published and reproduced with kind permission of Cambridge University Press.

Pages 40–41   Table 2: Approaches to needs analysis and their application to sampling for EAP assessment, adapted from Jordan, R.R (1997). *English for academic purposes: A guide and resource book for teachers*. Published and reproduced with kind permission of Cambridge University Press.

Page 45	Bloom's Taxonomy diagram reproduced from Bloom, B. S. (1956). *Taxonomy of educational objectives: The classification of educational goals. Handbook 1, Cognitive domain.* Reproduced with kind permission of Pearson Education, Inc., New York, New York.
Page 45	Bloom's Taxonomy diagram as updated by Anderson and Sosniak, reproduced from Anderson, L. W. & Sosniak, L. A. (1994). *Bloom's taxonomy: A forty-year retrospective.* Published and reproduced with kind permission of University of Chicago Press.
Page 61	Table 1: Steps in pre-testing, reproduced from Bachman, L. F. & Palmer, A. S. (1996). *Language testing in practice: Designing and developing useful language tests.* Published and reproduced with kind permission of Oxford University Press.
Page 72	Figure 2: A reflective EAP assessment research model, adapted from Gibbs, G. (1998). *Learning by doing: A guide to teaching and learning methods.* Published and reproduced with kind permission of Oxford Brookes University (Further education unit, OCSLD).
Page 81	Text from the Department for Children, Schools and Families (DCSF). © Crown Copyright 2008. Contains public sector information licensed under the Open Government Licence v3.0.
Page 82	Table 1: Features of good assessment for learning, adapted from Department for Children, Schools and Families (DCSF). © Crown Copyright 2008. Contains public sector information licensed under the Open Government Licence v3.0.
Page 94	Table 2: Characteristics of text usefulness, reproduced from Bachman, L. F. & Palmer, A. S. (1996). *Language testing in practice: Designing and developing useful language tests.* Published and reproduced with kind permission of Oxford University Press.
Page 107	Table 1: Measurement scales, adapted from Brown, J. D. (1998). *Understanding research in second language learning: A teacher's guide to statistics and research design.* Published and reproduced with kind permission of Cambridge University Press.
Page 143	Text reproduced from Kunnan, A. J. (2003). Test Fairness. *European Year of Language Conference.* CUP, 2003. 27. Print. © UCLES University of Cambridge Local Examinations Syndicate.
Page 163	Table 1: Characteristics of standardized tests, adapted from Davies, A., Brown, A., Elder, C., Hill, K., Lumley, T. & McNamara, T. (1999). *Dictionary of language testing.* Published and reproduced with kind permission of Cambridge University Press.
Pages 164–165	Table 2: Evolution of TOEFL tests, reproduced from ETS. *TOEFL program history.* Copyright © 2011 Educational Testing Services. All rights reserved. https://www.ets.org/s/toefl/pdf/toefl_ibt_insight_s1v6.pdf.
Page 165	Text from Foucault, M. (1977). *Discipline and punish: The birth of the prison.* Published and reproduced with kind permission of Penguin Books Ltd and Random House LLC.

Page 169	Table 3: The history of IELTS, adapted from Davies, A. (2008). *Assessing academic English: Testing English proficiency, 1950–1989 – the IELTS solution*. Published and reproduced with kind permission of Cambridge University Press.
Page 169	Table 3: The history of IELTS, adapted from IELTS. (2012). *The history of IELTS*. Reproduced with kind permission of IELTS.org and retrieved from: http://www.ielts.org/researchers/history_of_ielts.aspx.
Page 169	Table 3: The history of IELTS, adapted from Knapp, K., Seidholfer, B. & Widdowson, H. G. (2009). *Handbook of foreign language communication and learning*. Published and reproduced with kind permission of De Gruyter Mouton.
Pages 169–170	Table 4: Ingram's concerns about the use and misuse of IELTS, reproduced from Ingram, D. (2005). *English language problems in Australian universities*. [Radio broadcast]. Lingua Franca. Reproduced with kind permission of ABC Commercial.
Page 172	Table 5: Comments on the launch of PTE Academic, reproduced from Chung, J. (2009). *Pearson plans to release English proficiency exam to rival TOEFL*. Reproduced with kind permission of The Daily Pennsylvanian and retrieved from: http://www.thedp.com/article/2009/10/pearson_plans_to_release_english_proficiency_exam_to_rival_toefl.
Page 172	Table 5: Comments on the launch of PTE Academic, reproduced from Swain, H. (2012). *Patrick McGhee, new chair of Million+ thinktank, is trending nationally*. Reproduced with kind permission of The Guardian and retrieved from: http://www.theguardian.com/education/2012/may/07/patrick-mcghee-chair-millionplus-thinktank.
Page 172	Table 5: Comments on the launch of PTE Academic, reproduced from Stewart, W. (2009). *Essays to be marked by 'robots'*. Reproduced with kind permission of TES and retrieved from: http://www.tes.co.uk/article.aspx?storycode=6023725.
Page 181	Figure 1: Kolb's Cycle applied to EAP assessment, adapted from Kolb, D. A. & Fry, R. (1975). Toward an applied theory of experimental learning. In C. Cooper (Ed.), *Theories of group processes*. Published and Reproduced with kind permission of John Wiley & Sons Ltd.
Page 181	Figure 1: Kolb's Cycle applied to EAP assessment, adapted from Kolb, David. A., *Experimental learning. Experience as the source of learning and development*, (1st ed.), © 1984, p. 42. Reprinted by permission of Pearson Education, Inc., New York, New York.